2. October 2012

Sister Mary

Bringing you greetings
from Ireland on our
visit to the USA.
Your Loving Cousins
Hugh + Mary.

WHERE GOD HIDES

WHERE GOD HIDES

A JOURNEY OF DIVINE AWAKENING

Liam Lawton

HACHETTE
BOOKS
IRELAND

First published in 2012 by Hachette Books Ireland
A division of Hachette UK Ltd.

A CIP catalogue record for this title is available from the
British Library.

ISBN 978 144474314 2

Inside design and typeset by Bookends Publishing Services.
Cover design by AmpVisual.com.
Cover author photo by Donal Norton

Printed and bound in Great Britain by
CPI Group (UK) Ltd, Croydon, CR0 4YY

Hachette Books Ireland policy is to use papers that are
natural, renewable and recyclable products and made from
wood grown in sustainable forests. The logging and
manufacturing processes are expected to conform to the
environmental regulations of the country of origin.

Hachette Books Ireland
8 Castlecourt Centre
Castleknock
Dublin 15, Ireland
A division of Hachette UK Ltd
338 Euston Road
London NW1 3BH

www.hachette.ie

CONTENTS

For my parents
Tom and May

There is a time for everything

And a season for every activity under the heavens:

A time to be born and a time to die
A time to plant and a time to uproot,
A time to kill and a time to heal,
A time to tear down and a time to build,
A time to weep and a time to laugh
A time to mourn and a time to dance,
A time to scatter stones and a time to gather them
A time to embrace and a time to refrain from embracing
A time to search and time to give up
A time to keep and a time to throw away
A time to tear and a time to mend
A time to be silent and a time to speak
A time to love and a time to hate
A time for war and a time for peace .

ECCLESIASTES 3:1–8

INTRODUCTION

I am often asked why I chose the way of life that I live and also often challenged about the certainty of what I believe in. In our world of constant change, challenge and unpredictability, one thing has never wavered for me: my belief in God.

How God communicates is not as obvious as we would like to think, but nevertheless for me is very real and at times most consoling. There are times when it is also very challenging, as I struggle to locate His presence in times of crisis, when it can feel remote or obscured from view. God hides in the most unusual and unexpected places and will reveal Himself when we least expect it.

Sometimes in the simplest of ways God's presence and love is revealed to me and I find myself marvelling at the beauty of the divine imagination. One of the means of communication is the sacred scriptures found in the Bible. People have their own favourite passages or lines and one such passage that I constantly return to is from the Book of Ecclesiastes. Here the author writes of a natural cycle and rhythm to life. It is within this cycle or framework that I believe God is found and reveals his different faces, often when we least expect. These lines form the basis of this book – an exploration of divine revelation in ordinary human lives and experiences. All of the lives mentioned have touched my own life, some in an extraordinary way and others in ways that will never be known. I have found God hiding, sometimes camouflaged in the natural beauty of our planet, or the God of great joy, found in the poorest slums of Africa or the healer who is revealed in the Mayan foothills of Guatemala, or in the prisons of Pakistan or in a chance meeting in a Dublin suburb.

These stories and many more reveal a very different face of God who does not interfere with human living but instead enters into the very depth of it and becomes present to those who wish for 'eyes to see, and ears to hear'. They are stories of pain and beauty, stories of challenge and consolation but above all stories of inspiration. Somewhere even now, God is being revealed – not in any devious manner but in humble ways that need time to unearth themselves and be discovered. It is in great simplicity that great beauty is revealed, and maybe then and only then can we discover where God truly hides.

A TIME TO
BE BORN

Lord

You knew me before

You entrusted me to this earth

Calling me

To where I am

That I might take my place

Among gentle souls

That would gaze upon my eyes

And smile in sweet surprise at

The legacy of likeness of older generations

May I bring new dreams from your place of eternity

Where each birth holds boundless possibilities

To bless us with your grace

The mystery of each future

Reveals anew your face.

I am trying to decipher the notes of birdsong that are emanating from the tree outside my window. It's been the pleasant background sound for the past few days in this early springtime. In secret and through the glass window, I have watched my feathered friend build a new home on the branch of a poplar tree. Many painstaking journeys have been made to gather the bits and pieces that have formed the outline of a nesting place. A little beak perching high on the tall tree can emit beautiful notes but can also carry the muck and mud of a future home that will give shelter, rest and comfort on dark stormy nights or warm summer evenings. I feel I have new neighbours, and yet I know so little about *them*!

Hopefully building the nest will be followed by courtship and nesting, the laying of eggs and the eventual hatching of new life – and then, new song! As the building continues, I watch the intricate dangling of twigs and branches, the consolidation of walls with pockets of mud and the eventual padding with designer moss, the envy of any estate agent! Why this little thrush has decided to nest in my garden I have no idea – perhaps it is just coincidence that the tall trees growing there offer an impatient bird a safe haven to nest, or perhaps this experience has been given to me so that I might reflect a little on my own place, my own sense of belonging.

As someone who believes deeply that the divine imagination of God is constantly unfolding before us, I marvel at the worlds within worlds that exist before and around us that so often mirror our own desire for survival and our need to belong. In time, this little nest will become the shared space where shelter and survival will go hand in hand. Where the inhabitants will be beak-fed before, in time, learning to find their own way and their own food – or perish in hunger. From here, my feathered friends will be pushed from the loft of cosy comfort to take flight into the vista of limitless space under two tiny wings.

The miracle of life and the innate desire to reproduce rests at the heart of all species of life, and we are no different. The instinct to belong and survive is as strong and important in big and small creatures alike, human or otherwise.

Each of us is born into a particular time, place and family, which nurtures our desire for living and enhances our deep desire to belong. In the twenty-first century, the meaning of the term 'family' has changed significantly, but no matter what shape a family takes, we still have a great hunger to be part of a kinship that bestows security, affection and love upon us. At certain times when such kinship is threatened by danger, illness or even death, our limitations and fragility come to the fore, but so too does our sense of duty and our sense of loyalty, giving truth to the saying: 'Blood is thicker than water.'

Every place has its own characteristics that influence those who dwell there. Many places have a language of their own and particular ways or life or rituals that mark the boundaries between it and another place. You can sometimes tell where someone is from by virtue of their language and dress code, even before you know anything about them. What is native within us will almost always remain, even if we move far away from home and settle in a distant land.

I recall being in a settlement in the USA – Springfield Massachusetts – where people had moved some generations back from the south of Ireland. If I closed my eyes while I listened to them speak, I could imagine that they had never left their original home place. Economic circumstance had brought them to a particular place, but they were still deeply rooted in the culture that they had left behind, their sense of identity was still very much bound up in a particular way of life.

People's identity can become even stronger when they move from the security of their home environment. This is especially true when people have been forced to leave their home place because of a lack of economic opportunities. These emigrants will try to make a home away from home to bring some sense of familiarity and normality to their otherwise unfamiliar surroundings.

How often do we visit houses and see the family photographs or local landmarks of the place they have left behind festooning the walls? In the area of the Midlands where I come from, there is a well-known saying: 'You can take the man out of the boglands, but you can't take the boglands out of the man.' It is as if our DNA connects us to our landscape and remains instilled in our psyche.

It is 'home' that offers us comfort, courage and consolation at the different stages of our lives. The buildings in which we live may be merely structures, but they house the furniture of emotion – love, affirmation, encouragement as well as the counter emotions of anger, bitterness and sadness. Such emotions are the real signs of a lived-in home. A home may be full of material possessions but lack the real ingredients of living – it is not so much the inhabitants that are missing but the true emotions that bind a family or people together.

Sadly, in these days of great economic uncertainty, it is also not uncommon to drive through the countryside and see new houses uninhabited, a stark reminder of a different era that suggested unending affluence, but also perhaps, in their lonely state, a stark reminder of the loss of community and kinship, and the security of being surrounded by people who know, accept and love us for who and what we are.

Economic uncertainty has once again ripped through families and communities, causing great stress, anxiety and insecurity. So many people, who until relatively recently lived comfortable carefree lives, find themselves in social welfare queues or suffer silently as they watch their meagre savings disappear before their disbelieving eyes. For some people, the difficulties of becoming so vulnerable in the light of changed life circumstance have proved too much, as the suicide statistics only too painfully remind us.

We are each born into a specific time, place and people, but our true identity is more than the sum of these elements combined. We each belong to the divine God who created us and who is constantly making conversation at the deepest level with us. Our search in life, though we may not consciously know it, is our search to find God, because in Him lies our true place of belonging.

We can spend our whole lives searching for fulfilment, failing to see that God who created us constantly invites us to be in a relationship with Him. This invitation is often manifested in our need to belong. This divine longing has been with us since we were born and is expressed in so many different ways – in our personalities, our thoughts and our actions lie the deep desire and longing for union with God, though we may seldom recognise it. And because we don't recognise our relationship with God, we search for fulfilment elsewhere. Then, when our desires are not met, we move to searching elsewhere, sometimes with increased intensity, and we become more disappointed when our needs remain unmet.

In today's world, there is much emphasis on image, material gain and success. We can spend every waking hour chasing such dreams in the belief that fulfilling them will make us happier. As we search unendingly to quench our desires, we create a world where selfishness and gratification become acceptable norms, and conditions such as isolation and loneliness, that were unheard of in previous generations, cause great suffering and human misery. These conditions that are so prevalent in contemporary society can hinder our ability to connect with God, who longs to find a home within us and offer hope, security and genuine love.

How many people live medicated lives because they are unable to face the reality of aloneness or because their lives do not live up to the unrealistic expectations that they themselves have set? How many of us have imprisoned ourselves within invisible walls that grow higher and higher as we continue to seek an illusion of happiness that only leads to further isolation and unhappiness? This might paint a depressing picture and yet true freedom comes from acknowledging where we are now and how we got here. Those who are prepared to ask these questions have begun to discover that where there is true honesty and courage, there is hope.

I have always been fascinated by the Christmas

story of the visit of the Magi – the 'outsiders' who came in search of a new star that appeared on the horizon and ended up kneeling in homage at the foot of a baby's cradle. I have always been deeply moved by the poems of T.S. Eliot, especially 'The Journey of the Magi' and the striking images portrayed in verse of oriental camels, snow-strewn roadsides and busy taverns. Despite the deception of Herod's hospitality and all the trappings offered with it, their instinct enables them to acknowledge humbly the birth of Jesus, God's son, but also enables them to decide to take a new and different route home. They had come in search of greatness, majesty and power, but what they found was so vastly different: a child in a stable, not a prince in a palace. And so their lives were never the same again.

We are like Magi in our own worlds – searching and seeking, but uncertain about what or for whom we search. For some, the journey has been too long; for others, it's only beginning. Many others have left the path on the journey; while others still have lost their way and feel isolated and alone. The simple stable in Bethlehem was a home in those midnight hours. Despite all its poverty and great deprivation in worldly affairs, it was rich beyond comparison in love, belonging, security and hospitality – all the qualities that answer our deepest longings. The poor shepherds, the wise travellers and astronomers who come to a Bethlehem manger, all recognised the presence of mystical beauty lying before them. This is what we need to discover, or even rediscover, in contemporary life – the supernatural dwelling among the natural, how God hides and dwells among us all.

The Irish tradition of placing a lighted Christmas candle in the window of the home as a gesture of welcome to strangers, as well as to light the way for Joseph and Mary on their way to Bethlehem, is a recognition of this dwelling of the supernatural among the natural. The stranger is offered hospitality because even the Lord Himself could appear in any guise or disguise, so we should always be ready to welcome Him. In Áras an Uachtaráin, since the time of Mary Robinson's presidency, there is a candle in a window that is lit permanently and which can be seen by passers-by in the Phoenix Park. It has been a symbol of welcome and hospitality through the years.

When we invite God into our lives, we bring to life the promise of Jesus from St John's Gospel – 'Make your home in me as I make mine in you' (John 15:4). How humbling and intimate is this promise from Jesus, that God, who humbled Himself to be born in Bethlehem, would also humble Himself to dwell within our lives? The God who hung the moon, who carved the Great Barrier Reef, who coloured the kingfisher, who composed the beautiful sound of rain and the song of the night owl, the God who created the tender laugh of a child and the lonely tears of a lover, the mystical words of poets and the chiselled hands of a labourer creating shelter, the God who knows every tiny bird that flies – even the one nesting in my garden – longs and desires deeply to rest within our hearts and our souls. How incredible is that?

When people cross the threshold of our being, we build relationships as we encounter the blessing of others in our lives. The more we encounter others, the more opportunities we have for growth and development, honesty and maturity. We learn to listen to what others can say to us and realise what they have to offer us, so that we, in turn, can offer support, love and affirmation to others. This is how we encounter God in our lives. We become less self-centred as we learn to listen to the needs of others. We learn to be honest. We learn to make choices. We learn that we don't have all the answers, that we have still much to learn. But we also realise that we are not alone. God is with us. God who makes *His* home within us will bring about transformation in our lives and bring us to new places where we truly belong.

The German writer Johann Wolfgang von Goethe once wrote: 'They are happiest, be they King or Peasant, who find peace in their homes.' There is a something very sacred about the places we inhabit. I have lived in my own community for a number of years and have always felt a sense of belonging among the kind and welcoming people. I am privileged to share the joys and sorrows, the good times and bad times with this community, and undoubtedly the life of each person has its influence on that of another. Because of my music, I travel a lot and there is always a sense of relief and rest when I return to my nesting place.

On one such occasion, I had been in Cork to perform at a charity event with my fellow musicians. When the concert was over, I felt too tired to drive the three hours home. My hosts offered me a bed for the night and, because I had no commitments the following morning, I gladly accepted. Following a very restful sleep, I left early to ensure that I would be home by midday. It was a beautiful day for travelling and I made good progress, even with stopping for a coffee break and to buy the daily newspaper. When I eventually reached my home, I gathered the rubbish in the car and went to the back of my home where the dustbin is kept. Then I noticed – the backdoor of my house was wide open. I admonished myself for not checking that the door had been locked before I'd left.

As I came closer to the door, I began to see some things strewn on the floor. The wind through the open door has knocked them over, I thought to myself. Then, and only then, did the real truth suddenly dawn on me as I walked into my kitchen.

My house was like a house that had been hit by a gale-force tornado. I stood in complete shock as I tried to take in the scene before me. Every cupboard, every drawer, was open with all the contents smashed and broken on the floor. I stepped over bottles, broken plates and opened the door leading into the hallway. Then I realised that the whole house had been ransacked. Every room, every cupboard, every bookcase was upturned and emptied. Broken furniture, broken glass and broken ornaments littered the hallway and the bedrooms. In my office, which I always tried to keep organised, I was met with a scene that was more akin to something from an Armageddon movie. All my files had been taken from the filing cabinet and emptied into a large pile in the middle of the floor. The bookshelves had been emptied and hundreds of sheets of music were strewn everywhere, and my books were dumped in heaps. One bookcase was broken in half and a beautiful hand-made pottery crucifix that I had got a few weeks previously from Assisi, lay broken on the floor.

As I walked numb and in silence through the house, I realised that there was more to come. Much had been taken from the house, including hundreds of music CDs that I had collected over the years, as well as all my own recordings – even those I was still working on. Years of work had vanished in minutes. My intruders had filled any cases and carrier bags they could find with anything that was of value and would sell.

Many things passed through my mind. The question 'why?' was one, but I was also aware of the other question – 'why not?' I had heard of similar things happening to others, so why should I be any different? Such thoughts did not, however, bring any consolation as I tried to cope with the scene before me. I remember praying for calm and for the courage to act in the best way. Not wanting to frighten my neighbours, I called the police first and then my brothers who, though some distance away, came right away. I still remember the face of the guard when he saw the result of my night visitation. For the rest of that day, the police and detectives worked at the scene. By evening, word had spread and I was immersed in the kindness of good friends and neighbours who were genuinely shocked and annoyed.

I found it difficult to come to terms with the loss of so much of my work, particularly material that was very personal to me. I had just completed a work in Symphony Hall, Chicago that had been narrated by the legendary screen actor Gregory Peck, and I had been given the master copies of the recording. It was one of the last public performances Gregory Peck made before he died, and he had agreed to narrate the work for me for a special St Patrick's night performance for the Irish community in Chicago. It was also the very first recording of any orchestral work that I had done, and so it was very personal and special for me. Now it was destined for some weekend market and a listener who would never know its value in personal terms.

By eight o'clock that evening, when the police had finished their investigations, I was allowed to begin the process of tidying. Obviously, the intruders had hoped to find money and had ransacked the house, spending a considerable amount of time in it as I had not come home. Perhaps it was fortunate that I had not. I would have arrived home very early in the morning and would probably have disturbed them.

Uncertain where to begin the clean-up, I began in the kitchen and then moved to the office. I tried to deal with the mixed emotions of anger and anxiety. I knelt on the floor of the office to begin sorting through the mountain of files that littered the room. As I lifted a bundle of files, I became aware that there were photographs emptied out on the floor too. Taking up the bundle, I began to look through them, suddenly I saw scenes from my life – family, friends, community events, people and occasions that I forgotten about or had not seen for a while. Sitting on the floor, I became totally immersed in the people and places before me and, in a moment of epiphany, I became aware of how fortunate I was. Despite the ugliness and the trauma of the day, I had things that no one could take from me – the love of family and friends, and the goodness and support of people whom I could always count on. These were real treasures that no one could ever steal from my heart. I may have had many material things stolen and things of sentimental value taken, but sitting on the floor in the midst of mayhem, I began to appreciate the important things in my life reflected in simple photographs, precious memories encased in a paper frame. I realised at the moment that I was indeed blessed despite everything. As I sat on the floor, I heard the doorbell ring. It was now dark outside and as I opened the door, I saw a young man standing there. I recognised him as being from the other side of town. He handed me a bottle of wine and simply said, 'We heard what had happened and we are very sorry.' I was very touched. I invited him in but he said, 'Not at all, we just wanted to let you know we were thinking of you.' And then he left.

In the days, that followed, I got my house back in order and thanks to the great dedication of the local police, my music was retrieved and my personal work was returned undamaged having been offered for sale for a pitiful sum – all good for my humility! But it was the random acts of kindness that enabled me to recognise the hidden compassion of God, revealed in the empathy of generous hearts. This was the gift that I received. And from dusty, faded photographs came a blessing that no thief in the night would ever steal.

A TIME TO
PLANT, A TIME
TO UPROOT

In the sound of distant voices
New horizons
Alluring choices
May we find an anchor
Solidly resting in our heart
Deeply rooted in your compassion
O God
And wherever we lay our heads
May we be held firmly
Knowing that
You go before us
And await on the other side of wonder
Planted and rooted in love
We shall never be afraid.

My grandmother was a young girl in 1912 when the Titanic sailed out of Cobh on its way to New York. Two years previously my grandfather had left for the US before returning to marry her and settle in the beautiful rustic, rolling hills of east Cork near Youghal Bay, in the townland of Ballymacoda. My grandmother was gifted with a beautiful voice and was well known in the area for singing at wakes and weddings, but also for singing what were known then as 'American Wakes', the gatherings of friends and family to say goodbye to loved ones before they emigrated.

Emigration had become the great and only option for thousands who longed for a better future for themselves and their families (or the families they hoped to have). Cobh was one of the main places of departure and became the place of a thousand tears as people bid goodbye to their loved ones. However, the departure began long before the emigrants left the port. It was ritualised in the American Wake. For many of those who were leaving, it would be the last time they would see their parents and loved ones – not only that, it would also be the last time they would hear their voices, since the telephone was not accessible to them. An account of a typical leave-taking comes from Kerry we read:

The American Wake began at night time, in the house of the emigrant, and continued through the night until the early hours. The young emigrant would have previously visited friends and neighbours letting them know of the impending departure. All who were close were expected to attend.

They often were not occasions for merriment, but sombre gatherings with serious conversation and advice for the young emigrant. In areas of acute poverty, no refreshments were offered, but on rare occasions, a few neighbours brought a small quantity of poteen, but generally the dancing was absent.

Women noted for their ability to keen (wail or lament) would be called upon to acquaint listeners with the virtues of the emigrant and the suffering brought upon the parents by the departure. This eulogy was given in a high-pitched wail, resulting in a room full of keening women and weeping men. For 'when money was scarce, travel slow and perilous, illiteracy widespread, and mail service highly uncertain and destinations only vaguely perceived, the departure for North America of a relative or neighbour represented as final a parting as a descent to the grave'.

In less poverty-stricken areas, the American Wake proved itself a more festive occasion. Baking, cooking and cleaning were all part of the preparations. Neighbours frequently contributed food and a half-barrel of porter or stout was available for the men. The kitchen furniture was moved and seating was provided around the walls for neighbours and friends. Song and dance followed, only to be interrupted by offers of tea, and stronger beverages. Jibs, reels, quadrilles, hornpipes and Irish step dancing were the order of the day. The older people seated themselves around the hearth, while the younger ones took to the floor.

The next morning, the emigrant was accompanied by friends and family to the train station or the dockside for his embarkation.

From *Blennerville, The Gateway to Tralee's Past,* Kelley, et al.

For those who lived away from Cobh, relatives and friends would accompany the emigrant to the railway station where there would be great lamenting and mourning as the person boarded the train and headed for Cobh (or Queenstown as it had been renamed after a visit by Queen Victoria in 1850). It is not difficult to imagine the thoughts of people boarding the trains and facing the long lonely sail across the Atlantic, never to see their homes and familes again.

It's now a hundred years since my grandfather emigrated and though communication technologies have made our world much smaller and more accessible, the pain of the human heart when saying goodbye is still very real. Recession has once more visited our shores and is tearing families and communities apart as people try to find a better future for their families. Over the past decade, our airports had become places of welcome and freedom, as people enjoyed the value of travel and home-coming, but now the world is a very different place and many people are being forced to leave the land, people and places they love. Sitting in airports, I cannot but observe the pain and frustration at the reality of having to leave loved ones and begin all over again – the pain of not only those leaving, but also of those who are left behind. Thankfully, there is not the same isolation as before and through things such as Skype and other means of communication it is possible to bring two worlds closer if only on a screen or telephone.

The loss of young, bright and talented people within our communities can never be underestimated. The lifeblood of any community is its young people who have so much to offer and indeed ensure the future of a community. When such people are forced to leave and make a life elsewhere, it leaves and indelible mark on the society they leave behind. Our loss is the gain of somewhere far away.

We can only hope that our people will find work, a welcome and a better future, but we also hope that conditions will improve so that these people can return to be with the people they know and love. The isolation and loneliness of families at such a time is probably never fully known; behind every door the heartache is private and at times silently suffered.

I recently sat in one such home and became acutely aware of the ticking of a clock. There are only so many words that you can say when the reality of aloneness becomes real. This was a mother whose two sons have emigrated and now there is no one at home with her ageing husband and herself. Gone are the dreams of grandchildren running home every day or the hours of babysitting about which grandparents dream, and should enjoy.

This is where I believe a Christian community has an important role to play, providing support and compassion to people who are lonely, isolated and fearful of the future. This is where we are called to share our time, gifts and prayers with all who know these sorrows. Many families have been affected, and it is still continuing each week.

And what of those who leave? The process of adapting to new surroundings, new work places, new people and new cultures can be daunting to say the least. The ability of individuals or families to cope with new and changing circumstances makes each person's and each family's experience of emigration unique. Very often, people lose their whole sense of identity when they move from a sheltered and secure environment to a place of anonymity. This can often impact on the mental health of those involved and, without doubt, can rupture relationships and cause serious strain. Dealing with 'homesickness' can bring huge pain and very often people, especially men, carry this burden in silence for the sake of their children and other loved ones.

In Chapter One, I wrote about the need to belong and how essential this is in all our lives. This need can be seriously undermined for those who emigrate as their sense of attachment to a familiar place called home is lost. This attachment offers security and sanctuary and, without it, we begin to feel very vulnerable – even though we know, deep down, that home no longer offers the same opportunities or a positive future. Such an acknowledgement can cause great turmoil and unease as people try to respond to their new circumstances.

Another impact that this separation brings is a sense of guilt. I have often met people who live abroad who are very conscious of the needs of their elderly parents or siblings still at home, and their almost desperate frustration at not being readily available to help and offer assistance when it is needed. Relationships within the families – both the nuclear family and the extended family – can change when one or more of the people within the family are working away. I recently spoke with a young father who had to find work abroad because of the economic climate. He returns home every three months for a weekend visit. I can only imagine the stress and strain on all sides as this family tries to maintain order and some semblance of normality in a situation that is fraught with stress and human loneliness. Such scenarios give rise to great isolation on every side.

There are many reasons why people emigrate, some more complex than others. Many young people take the time before they settle down in life to travel with a sense of adventure, but such circumstances are vastly different to the person who is forced to emigrate because of political, economic or social reasons.

'Culture shock' is the term given to the physical and emotional distress that comes from being away from your familiar environment and having your boundaries changed. It affects everyone who becomes involved with a new culture and it challenges our beliefs, values and practices. All the values and the normal traits of our culture are taken for granted at home, but in a new environment all that is secure is removed – and there are often casualties. How many people who simply want to fit in and live normal lives are rejected because of their skin colour or ethnicity? How many suffer the consequences of segregation and sectarianism just because they are from a particular race or creed?

In Ireland, figures released by the Central Statistics Office in September 2011 show that within the year of April 2010 and April 2011 almost 80,000 people emigrated from Ireland, with over half of these being Irish nationals. Many of these people have found work but there are many who are also undocumented and are constantly anxious about the vulnerability of their situations. Such people can never possess a driving licence, receive social welfare assistance or have proper medical care. If they ever come into conflict with the law, they are completely vulnerable and run the risk of being deported from the country and returned to their own place of origin and the circumstances they tried to escape.

The Christian response must always be to stand up for the fundamental human rights of all people. God does not discriminate based on accidental characteristics of our birth – that we are born in Ireland, Iran or Iceland is entirely out of our control as is the colour of our skin and the creed we have known since childhood. As Christians, we are challenged to meet all circumstances with human empathy and compassion treating all human beings regardless of background with the dignity and integrity they deserve. The Catholic Church directs us in this.

> *All people have a right to have their basic human needs met in their homelands.*
> *If their basic needs cannot be met in their homelands, persons have the right to seek them abroad.*
> *The right to migrate is not absolute and can be mitigated in favour of the common good.*
> *Nations may regulate borders to provide for national security, tranquillity and prosperity.*
> *The right to regulate borders is not absolute and regulations must promote the common good.*

Nations with the ability to accommodate migrants
should respond with generosity.
Families have the right to remain united.

There are many challenges that face those who emigrate today – even the term 'alien', used when referring to such people, denigrates human beings into something that is faceless and soulless. This completely contrasts with the words of the gospel:

I was a stranger and you made me welcome.
Matthew 25:35

In the Irish tradition, offering hospitality to the stranger is seen as a very important part of Christian living, as the notion that the Christ himself could appear at any given time under a different form or guise to seek generosity and shelter. Written into the tradition was the beautiful prayer-poem, which I later adapted in song form:

I saw a stranger yestereen
A soul I'd never ever seen, and bade him welcome
I put food in the eating place, drinking in the
   drinking place
And he prayed to God on high
And the lark sang a pretty song
Often, often comes Christ in a stranger's guise
Often, often see Christ in the stranger's eyes.

When we come together to pray, no one should be a stranger and our gathering should not be foreign to anyone. In God, there is no division and we are all equal. It is the place that should offer brotherhood and welcome, especially for those who have to live outside the safety net of society. All people, especially those who are weak and vulnerable, are a living sign of Christ's presence and need to be treated with dignity and respect, because there but for the grace of God goes any one of us, especially those of us who have been born into a comfortable and self-sufficient environment.

I have been fortunate in my life to live in a place of peace and safety where the rights of other human beings are respected but in my prayer each day, I remember and pray for God's blessing on those who work in service of others, offering help and assistance of every kind especially in dangerous circumstances, of which there are many in the world today. I am often moved and humbled when such people find my music and writings of some assistance in their public work or in their own private lives.

With the aid of modern technology, it is possible to become aware within minutes of situations that have erupted without warning and to bring the facts and experiences of people to a wider world, which can help a situation, or at times may hinder it, as was recently seen during the Arab Spring uprisings, as meetings and gatherings were sabotaged due to the hacking of personal email accounts.

There are times, however, when events unfold about which we have no knowledge and about which we learn only after they are over. At these times, we can but wonder that on a certain day as we were going about our daily business, others were facing the most acute terror.

I was made aware of this one day when, in a bundle of letters delivered to my home in Carlow, I noticed one that was post-marked from the nearby county of Wicklow. On opening the letter, I discovered that there was a second envelope enclosed, from the Missionary Sisters of St Columba at Magheramore in County Wicklow. The letter simply suggested that I should have what was enclosed. It was a letter from a friend Rebecca Conlon, a Columban Sister from Milltown Malbay in County Clare, smuggled out of Pakistan during the recent difficult times there.

Very curious, I opened the second letter and began to read. The address given on the page was Hydrabad. It was 2006 and the Islamic world was still reeling from the offensive 'Cartoon Controversy' which had caused great disturbance and anger in many countries. The cartoon, drawn by a Danish artist in 2005, had caused an instant, and seriously negative, reaction that had moved from nation to nation in the Islamic world, like tumbling dominoes. There were protests and riots all across it and Pakistan became a hotbed of reaction.

Rebecca, a Columban Sister from Milltown Malbay in County Clare, had written the letter hoping that it would reach home along with some others for family

and friends. She had found herself alone in Pakistan
and had soon become caught up in the tensions and
awful turmoil:

*Three weeks before the 'Cartoon Controversy'
occurred, I had a dream in which I was frantically
looking for my crucifix. I searched everywhere and
eventually found it. On awakening and prompted by
the dream, I put on my crucifix as I felt the dream
had a message for me! A few days later, I was sitting
by the computer when the phone rang. I answered
but there was no reply. However, there was music
and noise in the background and I listened and could
hear the words:*

*I called you to be my sign and everywhere you go,
my hand will follow you.*

You will not be alone.

*In all the danger that you fear, you'll find me very
near …*

*The Psalms that I was reading for my daily
reflection were giving me the same message. What
was it all about? Because many riots had erupted and
because of the tension, I was warned to stay indoors
by the police and NOT to venture out in case of
danger. Such incidents as the Cartoon Controversy
can incite and inflame emotions to the detriment of
all sides, rather than engage respectfully in dialogue,
so as to understand each other. Just then, the doorbell
rang and was answered by the watchman who looked
after the place for us. He opened the door to two*

young men who were paying a surprise visit from the mosque to deliver a copy of the Holy Qur'an to the 'resident' of the house. The watchman explained that we were Christians and therefore had no need of the Holy Book but the men insisted that it be delivered. Having the utmost respect for the Holy Qur'an and all sacred books of religious traditions, it was very important that it be accepted graciously and not get damaged or disrespected in any way, if so there would be serious consequences. Thankfully, but with great difficulty, the Holy Book was returned by the watchman intact to the hands of the bearers. Then they enquired about the nationalities of the residents, which seemed very suspicious given the circumstances.

The following morning there was another unexpected knock on the door by two other young men and this visit raised my suspicions even higher as they wanted to meet the resident of the house. On hearing this, a few concerned Christians came and informed me that the incident was serious and had to be reported to the police for protection. It was then that my heart started thumping. The incident was recorded and given to the police. I became more and more anxious and being a non-national began to feel very vulnerable. Then I had a visit from the Bishop of Hyderabad who obviously was becoming concerned for my safety and well-being. Little did I realise that I would see him the following day on the television visiting a community where two churches had been burned to the ground amid allegations made about the desecration of the Holy Qur'an. I made contact with the community at Sukker, where the atrocities had happened, to offer my support. They were terrified but were able to make a quick escape when the fires had started and the violence had erupted, and were very grateful that their lives had been saved. As I watched the continued TV coverage, looking at the churches engulfed in flames, I realised that it was coming closer and closer to home all the time. No wonder the bishop and the authorities were watching out for me. Fear invaded the bones of the Christian community all over the country. The Cartoon Controversy had fuelled feelings never experienced before between the Christian and Muslim communities. Within two weeks, churches were burned, Christian schools and hostels were attacked, and so began one of the worst periods of persecution in the country's sixty-year history.

How does one get beyond the chaos and fear of this event? I remembered Rumi, the great Afghan mystic from this part of the world who once said:

Out behind ideas of right and wrong, there
is a field
I'll meet you there.

A number of my Pakistani friends, both Muslim and Christian, offered help and a safe haven to me during those terrifying days but, being European, I didn't want to draw trouble for them, so I stayed on my own, praying and trusting in God. It was unsafe to try and leave, so, staying in the basement, I relied on the watchman to bring food and to keep a close eye on all who might call. The fear of reprisal or of being burned out was constant. I was alone in the house with a curfew imposed on me night and day. In the house, there was a small chapel with a tabernacle where the Blessed Sacrament was reserved and there in the silence I beseeched God for His protection and His calm.

It was during these days of imprisonment that I had time to reflect on many things that I was usually too busy to think of. Recently, another Irish sister, en route from Ireland to the Philippines, had called and brought me some provisions which I now had time to savour and unwrap. News and gifts from home became a lifeline in the days that followed. Throughout the days and nights I read the letters and listened to some music, all instilling encouragement and hope as the words engraved on the ring that I have worn since the day I was professed many years ago – I will be with you always.

Hidden in the somewhat safety of the house, I waited, I prayed, I listened and I was also carried by the thoughts and prayers of my family, friends and my Columban congregation worldwide. A statement was issued by the bishops in Pakistan which included the words:

"No doubt, the violent attacks and desecration of our churches in Sanga Hill and Sukker and other incidents have greatly shocked our faithful and

*made them feel insecure and fearful of the future.
We once again condemn the offensive cartoons that
have hurt our Muslim brethren, and also deplored
the irresponsible mob violence and destruction of
private property.*

*May the words of dear Jesus Christ, 'Do not be
afraid ... Lo, I am with you till the end of time', fill
you with comfort, courage and peace!"*

Rebecca wrote of how music had helped her in times
of darkness, assuring her that God was by her side. She
cited a piece of mine called 'As You Go':

*I walked in the footsteps of the Cross with the
suffering church of Pakistan fearful and yet felt the
support and love of all who carried me in prayer.
I experienced the hidden, silent accompaniment
of my Muslim friends who worried for me in my
predicament. I sat in Rumi's field which lay behind
the right and wrong of the situation and faced the
dawn of a new beginning, knowing that life and my
sense of being and call to mission in Pakistan calls
for a radical witnessing to Jesus in spite of dangers
that might surround us, but living anchored in the
assurance of His presence, as echoed in the words of
'As you Go':*

> *Can you hear my promise*
> *Remembering your fear*
> *As you go into the dark*
> *I am somewhere near.*

After sometime, Rebecca and her companion left the house without being harmed and eventually arrived back in Ireland. We sat and talked for hours but I realised that her heart was still with the people of Hydrabad where she has returned to work in the women's prison and in the community.

I marvel at her ability to see beyond the fear of danger and recognise the goodness that exists in the hearts of these people. It's only when we walk in another's shoes that we truly come to know the other side of the story but it also gives us a great appreciation of how things are on the other side of life.

A Time
to Heal

I saw
A red tulip
Standing in the garden
Tall and firm
After winter's long reign
Straining toward the sunlight
That kissed its passion coat
Washed clean by spring rain ~

And I thought of your heart
Cleansed by daily suffering
Firm
Full to brim of rich love
To heal the invisible wounds
Carried and caused
By our daily living.

There is a great sadness in the world today. The soul of our beautiful world has been greatly wounded, and although we have reached technological heights and have conquered many of the limitations that held back previous generations, millions go to bed hungry every night and millions shed tears in loss and love hour by hour, day after day.

From Syria, we hear of untold heartbreak of innocent people, dying because of the ruthless, senseless greed and power of others. The Arab Spring that offered hope and transformation has become a night of endless sorrow for many. In the USA, millions are living in abject poverty, with little or no health protection. In Greece, so many more are now homeless in a country that was once the cradle of civilisation. In the horn of Africa, life expectancy is very short, with many children not living past their first year because of famine and starvation.

Here, at home in Ireland, the heartbreak of emigration once again haunts our shores as we watch thousands of our talented young people leave this land in search of a better future. This is the universal picture of a world in turmoil and hurting deep within. There are also the local situations, that we can come face-to-face with each day. The child who hungers in a cold home; the woman who cannot face looking at her emaciated face during chemotherapy; the young man who struggles daily with the darkness of depression but who cannot reveal his deep pain to the ones he loves; the young girl whose body is wracked with tremors in need of methadone; the old man who spends the day staring out of the window at strangers passing by, numbed by loneliness; the man whose inner child still weeps and wakes in dreams of former abuse; the priest who feels so inadequate as he tries to console the mother whose son has just taken his life ... the list goes on and on, day after day. Suffering visits all places, at all times without selection.

With suffering comes fear. Fear paralyses, fear breeds fear, fear destroys. There is nothing as isolating as suffering. It is all-consuming, and can leave someone raw and very exposed. The more we fight back, the more fearful we become. It is often very difficult to understand the logic or reason behind why such an outrage has been visited on us, or our family. Why should life treat us like this? Are we not deserving of something much better?

We can feel forsaken, as if God and life has forgotten us and has left us to find our own way in a darkened place. The same can be said of universal suffering – suffering within nations, cultures or groups of people.

You have only to think of the Jewish people in the Second World War, the Tutsi of Rwanda, or the peoples of Iraq or Palestine. We find it difficult to understand how such atrocities could happen as we consign such terrible happenings to memory. As John O'Donohue wrote in his book *Eternal Echoes*:

> *The suffering of a people is forgotten; they become faceless, mere ciphers of a trend or dynamic of history. To sanitise history is to blaspheme against memory. Equally, to become obsessed with the past is to paralyse the future.*

Suffering shifts the ground from under us. It can leave us in free-fall anxiety, as the world we know disappears and is replaced by a world of confusion and unknowing, especially when we are bereaved or separated from a loved one for one reason or another. When struggles limit our world, we begin to wonder how we will survive – the first day without a loved one, the first treatment for our cancer, the first night in prison, the first day on social welfare. Day becomes night and night will never end, like an endless winter.

It will always be very difficult to accept suffering, especially when we feel its burden is too heavy to carry. Even Jesus, the Son of God, was overwhelmed by the suffering he saw around him. I am always moved that the shortest sentence in the Bible – which gives the account of the raising of Lazarus with the words 'Jesus wept' – is also the most powerful. These two words are imbued with so much humanity and compassion and offer a great insight into the empathy of Jesus, the Son of God.

In the gospels, so many people desire to come to Jesus when they are overwhelmed by their own struggles or by those of the people they love. Such struggles may be of a physical nature or an emotional hurt or something even more sinister that haunts them and makes their life a living hell. Sound familiar?

When we see so much suffering around us, we can become paralysed by it all. Such feelings can cause impotence and guilt to take hold of us and we begin to feel worthless and helpless. The more I want to bring healing and hope to the world, the more I must not allow the dark forces to pull me down and paralyse my power within. I could easily become a victim of such forces, but instead I must keep my eyes focused on what's good, wholesome and compassionate. Thus a relationship with our creator, who is full of love and compassion, offers me hope, so that I can offer the same light to others around me.

When the Dalai Lama was asked about the Chinese who showed little love and kindness to his people in Tibet, he replied, 'They too are people who struggle to find happiness and deserve to find our compassion.' The Dalai Lama goes on to explain how he allows all the suffering of his people and their oppressors to enter into the depth of his heart, where it can be transformed into compassion.

I once met an old Irish Columban missionary who

had spent years in China and who had been imprisoned and tortured during the Chinese Revolution. He spoke kindly and caringly about the Chinese people, whom he had served and come to love. When I asked him about his time in captivity, he told me that during the months of his solitary confinement, he would pray and remember the prayers he had learned as a young boy in Ireland, and imagine what life was like back on the farm and in the village and the things he had learned as a boy. He said, 'I never took on the hate and fear that could have consumed my life. I conversed with God and He heard me – that, I believe, sustained me during those terrible days.'

Sometimes when we suffer, we prefer to walk the road of isolation. We want no one to know what we are enduring. To show any weakness would undermine us – heaven forbid that people would see us at our weakest. We prefer to keep our pain hidden so our loneliness goes unnoticed and the walls around us become higher and higher. We tell ourselves, 'I won't bother my friends, they have enough worries of their own and I don't want to be a burden.' But the truth is that we actually honour our friends by not hiding the truth from them and by allowing them to share our pain, as we in turn would expect them to share their pain with us. True, we cannot share our stories and our inner most struggles with everyone, but I believe that if we turn to God sincerely, he will place before us the people we need in such times – something I have often discovered in my own life.

Many times our pain is not just the result of external

conditions, but is also heightened by our sense of isolation and our inability to share with others. Some people will always find sharing very difficult, and will struggle immensely with unburdening their pain to another, but this is where hope can offer a light through a dark tunnel. This is the very basis of Christian belief – that we live our lives for and with others, embracing the blessings and the pain, the joys and the sorrows. Sometimes we need to take very small steps before we learn to entrust the sacred story of our lives to the heart of another but when we take those steps, we feel a new freedom as we give ourselves permission to begin a new journey of hope and healing. To tell another person 'I am lonely' or 'I need help' demands great courage, but if we trust in God's compassionate care for us, He will provide, of that I am certain.

In the natural world, winter's end will eventually come and from beneath the white earth, hardened by months of frost, a tiny crocus will emerge, vulnerable, fragile and alone against all the elements, but standing beautiful and straining towards the sunlight. Despite the harshness of our winters, the dwarf tulips in passion red dressings will flower and point to hope among the weeds of winter. New life will emerge but it may be different, very different. Our ability to embrace our suffering may be slow and very painful, but it may offer a grace that brings new fortune, new moments of life – not just because of a new future but also from a wisdom we bring from our past, the learned lessons of life.

Very often when we suffer, we have to let go of the

things that we cherish most – a loved one, a job, our standing in society, our physical appearance, even our name or identity. Learning to let go of such treasures demands great will and determination, and is not easy. Suffering can be a very lonely place. Talk to anyone who has had to brave the world after losing a partner and you will realise how isolated people can be. We may wish to hide away and throw the key to oblivion, but painfully and slowly we must take the first steps of embracing a different path that will eventually take us to a new, if different, world.

On such a road, the support of fellow travellers can offer much courage and help as we set out to walk again into the light. Such light will come through the compassion of others. I have benefited from this compassion and, in time, I hope I can offer the same humanity, compassion, care and understanding to the broken people I meet in my own life. Compassion means a willingness to come close to someone who suffers, but it also entails a willingness to show our own vulnerability. To show compassion means leaving our propensity for judgement outside. This is a place where tears are shared – otherwise it is not compassion, it's pity, and there is a great difference between pity and compassion.

Only when I am aware of my *own* suffering – and only then – can I become aware and attentive to the brokenness of my sister or brother. How can I know what it's like to be poor if I am not aware of my own poverty? This is the time when we can also admit that perhaps we don't have *all* the answers but that perhaps the *only* thing we can offer is a listening presence, which is one of the greatest gifts of all. How many times have we acknowledged such times in our own lives when we have felt deep gratitude for the people who didn't bail out and leave us in our pain and isolation but who took the time and love to journey with us beyond the barricades?

As I write these words, I have just watched the funeral service of Whitney Houston, who was undoubtedly blessed with a most beautiful voice. Anyone on any continent could recognise her unique talent. She sold millions and millions of records and yet she died alone, broken and in deep pain. Would that we could rewind time and right the wrong the sad irony of someone who sang of the 'greatest love of all' dying so young, with still so much to give.

When we become aware of the misery of another, when we take the trouble to walk in their shoes, when we listen with a listening heart, then we know something about the heart of Jesus and how He lived. I firmly believe, that if we turn to Him in the silence of our own hearts, God will replenish our spirits so that we can bring His love and His compassion to another.

A pure heart create for me O God, put a steadfast spirit within me. Do not cast me away from your presence, nor deprive me of your holy spirit.

Psalm 51

One of the most striking examples of embracing God's love and not giving in to negativity that I experienced was in 2008, when I travelled with two friends to the heart of the Kenyan bush, to the village of Nu, near the settlement of Mwingi, a town in the country's eastern province. It has an urban population of about 10,000 people and is situated 200 miles from Nairobi. We had reached Mwingi on market day and the open square was a mass of bodies and colours engaged in commerce and daily life. Makeshift stalls stood row by row alongside each other with various items for sale ranging from poultry, coffins and second-hand clothes, mixed with the dust of barefooted children running freely around the market. My sense of smell was assaulted with so many different scents but particularly by the smell of blood from slaughtered animals, drying in the heat of the sun. We bought our supplies of potatoes, bottled water and some other kitchen commodities, before we began our long trek into the heart of the bush, the unpaved roads seriously testing the small Land Rover we had hired for the journey. In the two and a half hours, we travelled into the bush, we passed no one on the road and were able to immerse ourselves in a beautiful isolation in the company of sunbirds who darted in and out of the wild bush looking for careless termites.

As a boy, I had often escaped the humdrum of Irish life by watching many episodes of *Tarzan*, as he came to settle and befriend the local villagers, having found himself abandoned in an African bush. Always lurking somewhere was the unknown and the definite sense of adventure. Now I was in the *same* land and seeing the bougainvillea and mango trees that had once been mere black and white TV images from another era.

Mutanu, as she is locally known, is an Irish Sister of

Mercy from west Cork and is the reason for our visit. Sr Gorretti Ward, who lived and worked as nursing sister in Carlow, decided to complete her life by working with and among the people of eastern Kenya. She works at a local clinic and supports its programmes, but has especially pioneered ophthalmic treatment with the aid of Irish volunteers who spend a number of months each year treating patients in various centres and clinics and ensuring that many people have their sight restored. It's been a remarkable achievement.

She has asked us to accompany her farther into the bush to visit a family she has been attending. They are one of the many who eke out a living out of clearing wild vegetation to sow maize and other such crops. The sun climbs higher into the noon sky and the flies buzz in loud chorus. Our skin is sweet and different. The rains have not come for months and a dried up riverbed acts like a sand-filled motorway. We drive slowly and determinedly through the rough vegetation. Here and there, people stop in the fields and wave to us. It does not go unnoticed by my friends that it is the women whom we see working in the fields, harrowing the dry earth and watering the soil with old buckets and plastic containers.

The road ends suddenly, and we cannot drive any farther, we must travel the rest of the way on foot. I marvel at how Mutanu, who grew up in the wilds of west Cork, finds her way with ease. I watch for snakes in the undergrowth. After a time, I hear voices but can see no one. Suddenly a little girl comes running, barefooted and cries out to Mutanu. From the sounds she is making, I realise she is deaf. The tattered summer dress is probably the only dress she has worn for years. She looks about nine years old, but could be older. Her beautiful dark hair is yellowing, which is typical of an undernourished child, but her face is alive with welcome. She is followed by her brothers and sisters all ages and sizes, all barefoot. One of the young boys clings to an old toy that seems almost too simple for his age and yet he holds it as if it were priceless. Nuvi, their mother, arrives. She is small in stature but offers a huge and demonstrative welcome to Mutanu and is oblivious to the rest of us. Nuvi is younger than I am, but has already given birth to nine children. Mutanu tells us that Nuvi's husband died almost two years earlier from an AIDS-related illness, like many of the villagers. Thankfully Nuvi has remained healthy and unaffected. Her joy is infectious as she welcomes us and introduces us to her children. Before long, I feel my hand gripped and, looking down, I see a smiling face urging me to come and see. I follow and watch the children thrashing maize heads with log rods to separate kernels. It's difficult work and I am uncertain about what to do, much to their amusement.

Their home, typical of an African rural home, is made from wattle and clay, with no running water, no electricity, and no toilet or no washing facilities. It is very primitive and stark and is a dwelling for Nuvi and nine children. As we round the corner, I notice two older girls who did not come to meet us. They are sitting in the dusty yard. One of them is holding a small baby in her arms. I ask Mutanu who the girls are, and I am surprised to learn that they are also Nuvi's daughters, both around sixteen or seventeen. As I get closer, I realise that neither of the girls can walk as their limbs are affected by disability. Neither girl can speak but their smiles are beautiful. Mutanu calls me aside and whispers their story. In utter disbelief, I hear how both girls were brutally raped by some local men – for one of the girls, it was the second time – and, as a result, each gave birth to a child, both of whom were now healthy babies.

Mutanu gazes into the distance and says, 'On the night that one of the children was born, the young brother ran the whole way into the village, miles away. His sister was in trouble he said and needed help. But because he did not have enough money for a hackney car, the driver refused to go and collect his sister, so thankfully he banged on our door late that night and we went out with him and eventually brought the poor girl in to deliver her baby. She was so frightened and ignorant to what was going on, but the baby was born safely. Soon after the other poor girl delivered her baby.'

I look around and see a healthy child sitting with a snotty nose and some wild bees buzzing nearby – too near for my comfort, so I lift the child into a safer place much to the amusement of Nuvi. I smile, but inside I am trying to grapple with indignation and anger at the vulnerability of this family and the inhumanity of the scene that has been relayed to us. I have rarely seen so much suffering within the confines of a family and yet they had a touching humility that left me disarmed.

Nuvi brings us to see the crop they are harvesting,

which will provide their staple diet and hopefully some surplus to sell at the local market. Again I am silenced when she tells us that her eldest son, who is fourteen years old but looks like a young boy of eleven, guards the crop at night for fear of armed thieves who could come to steal their food. I wonder how such a young and innocent child could protect himself, his crop and his family against any intruder. The wild trees and menacing scrub seem to concur. We walk to a grave surrounded by a small concrete lip. This is where Nuvi's husband was buried. The sadness of his absence is tangible.

The little girl who is deaf is watching us from a distance and Nuvi beckons her to come forward. Taking the child by the hand, she begins to clap her hands and dance. The little girl suddenly begins to follow suit, moving slowly to the mother's rhythm. The dusty yard rises as mother and daughter laugh loudly in each other's arms. Nuvi pulls Mutanu's arm and pleads with her to join with them. She throws her head back and laughs heartily embarrassed at our presence. It's almost a Brian Friel *Dancing at Lughnasa* moment, as the cares of the day are lost in a spontaneous dance. But this *is* Africa and we are many miles from home.

When our visit is over, we return to the bush and continue our journey by foot. As we take our leave, Nuvi is clinging to the arm of Mutanu and is still singing. She thanks us for coming to visit, and says, 'Thank you, thank you, for bringing an angel to us.' She places her arms around Mutanu's neck and embraces her. As we walk through the bush, I look behind. Closely following is the little girl who is deaf. She is smiling now and playing hide and seek in the undergrowth, a beautiful innocence permeates her face.

It is difficult to grasp the enormity of what we have seen. It is difficult to understand why so much human misery could be visited on such innocent ones, how human hearts could carry such suffering. But I also saw the depth of human affection that had reached into the deepest of wounds and had healed them with profound love. Perhaps the God who hides appears in the guise of the angel who comes with a simple reassuring smile, a gesture, or a small bag of food. In the midst of great suffering, there is great love.

Early in the evening, the night sky appears and the sun fades for another day. The stars in their thousands appear like diamonds, glistening over the silver night dew. I cannot close my eyes without seeing Nuvi settling her children to sleep in their mud hut, and her young son watching over their meagre crops in case of night thieves. May they be safe and sleep under your watchful eye, O Lord.

I cannot finish writing these lines without acknowledging the kindness and great generosity of my friend Peter who travelled with me and who later made it possible to provide Nuvi with a new concrete home for her children. Truly an angel had come to visit and help them heal.

A TIME
TO LET GO

In
Autumn
Stands the tree
Elegant and tall
Canopy of Gold
Surrenders to the Fall
Where ravens built a home
In evening light concealed
The wind blows from the north
Besieging falling leaves

Yet the tree it stands
Rooted deep and firm
No storm will ever shake
Its anchor deep within

Would life be but the same
If we could so divest
The trappings of our greed
The addictions of our quest

Simplicity in life
Simplicity in need
The secret of our life ~
A saintly, humble creed.

The nineteenth-century American writer and philosopher Henry David Thoreau once remarked that no man went down in his estimation because he had a patch in his trousers. His philosophy, based on his great respect and belief in the simple life, was condemned by the public, who were focused on image and the latest fashions. From his home by Waldon Pond in Connecticut, Thoreau practised the values of living simply and modestly, and he learned to appreciate the real beauty that surrounded him. His lived his life with the understanding: 'As you simplify your life, the laws of the universe will be simpler; solitude will not be solitude, poverty will not be poverty, nor weakness weakness.'

As recession begins to seriously affect all strands of society across the world, it seems that Thoreau's philosophy is gaining more respect. Sadly, we have lived our lives with standards that judged success by what people had rather than the type of people they were within. The more material possessions we amassed, the more important we believed we became. So if we wore something beautiful, which was admired by others, then we thought that we ourselves were being admired. Our value systems were determined by what we possessed rather than who we were.

We have come to see power and wealth in terms of material gain and those who have few worldly possessions often command very little respect. Throughout history, wars and battles have been fought over land, gold, diamonds, crops and human beings. The greed and self-gratification of some have caused so much pain and misery to others, and so it continues. But throughout history there have also been those who, against all odds and brutal force, have had the courage to give a *voice* to the voiceless. Francis of Assisi was one such person. Born into a noble and wealthy family, Francis began to realise that wealth would not bring inner fulfilment and happiness. His search for this fulfilment led him to believe that God was the source of our restlessness and ultimately we would only find true happiness when we emptied ourselves of all possessions and aspirations of wealth so that God could find a space in our lives.

Francis ritualised this by publicly removing his clothes and running through the streets of his native village naked, much to the great anger of his father and those who were close to him. Francis could see the abundant giving of God, which could never be enclosed in human constraints and was deeply moved by the lessons of Jesus, especially one from the Sermon on the Mount:

> *Do not worry about your life, what you will eat or drink; or about your body, what you will wear. Is not life more important than food and the body more important than clothes? Look at the birds of the air; they do not sow or reap or store away in barns, and yet your heavenly Father feeds them … And why do you worry about clothes? See how the lilies of the field grow: they do not labour or spin. Yet I tell you that not even Solomon, in all his splendour, was dressed like one of these. If that is how God clothes the grass of the field, which is here today and tomorrow is thrown into the fire, will he not much more clothe you, O you of little faith?*

The secret of Francis' life was his ability to be humble, so that God could become present. He saw his life as part of the overall creation of God, where the ordinary becomes the extraordinary. The essence of all creation is who we are in the eyes of God. Francis saw possessions as a barrier to being fully united with God:

> *If we had any possessions we should be forced to have arms to protect them, since possessions are a cause of dispute and strife, and in many cases we should be hindered from loving God and our neighbour. Therefore, in this life, we wish to have no temporal possessions.*

> Francis of Assisi

His own personal emptying of material possessions made him sensitive to those around him who lived in abject poverty, especially those who were outcast from society because of conditions such as leprosy. His desire to serve God removed Francis somewhat from the world in which he lived and yet by doing so, he became one of the greatest advocates for peace and justice that the world has known.

Francis saw great beauty in the ordinary things of life, simply because he took time to be aware of them. By reading his Canticle of Creation, we can see his great love and respect for a world imbued by the creativity of a beautiful mind – the mind of God.

Sadly, today, many people have made the world their 'god' and allowed it to determine the image of who we should be and how we should be rewarded if we live up to its demands. Such conditioning makes for great unhappiness as such fulfilment becomes unattainable for most people. How many people judge themselves against the standards placed before them on TV or in magazines or other social media. How many young people judge themselves unfairly, because they cannot measure up to their entertainment idols or their sporting heroes?

Somehow we tell ourselves that it's *not* okay to be ordinary. We need to be more than this. The real truth is that it's only when we are ordinary, when we are our real selves, that we are free. And such freedom gives others the space to be themselves too, without pretence, without masks. This is why people were drawn to

Francis of Assisi – it was his simplicity and ordinariness that enabled others to feel valued in his company. This was also the great gift of Jesus, who imbued those He met with a sense of their own worth and value. This is why His disciples followed him, why people were fascinated by His presence and why Mary of Magdalene walked into the pages of history by washing His feet with her tears. In His beautiful simplicity, she met herself:

> I tell you the truth, unless you become like little children, you will never enter the kingdom of Heaven.
>
> Matthew 18:3

Why is it so difficult for us to become ordinary and live more simple lives? True, most of us are being forced by some economic constraints to live less material lives but unless this comes with a change of heart or attitude about how we see life and ourselves, then we will remain imprisoned in a way of life that cannot bring ultimate fulfilment. Sometimes the more we have, the more we want, and we will keep wanting to fill our desires. But what we don't realise is that this need will never be fully satisfied. The bird that perches on the branch outside my window has nothing but a nest. Yet she is free to fly wherever she likes, whenever she likes – to the dancing river beyond my house, to the loft heights of the poplar trees, to the park at the other side of town, to the hills, miles away where purple heather and yellow furze colour a beautiful country canvas.

Living a more simple life is really about our attitude

and how we see the world. If we have expectations that live out of a materialistic need, then it will be more difficult to let go of our perceived need for possessions. If, on the other hand, we can learn to need less and value what we do have, then we can begin to live in a more simple way, uncongested by the distractions of the material world. Slowing down and stopping in our tracks will enable us to take stock and evaluate what is important to us. If we can do this and begin to declutter our lives, we will find that we have room for other important issues. The non busyness, the time for ourselves, can become time given to God and to others. In all religious traditions, such time is much valued because it enables a person to develop a relationship with the god of their belief system. For Christians, such time is the beginning and the essence of contemplation. When barriers and distractions are removed, there is room for God.

I like to think that each day we can, in some way, immerse ourselves in the mystery of God. What does this mean? The ancient Celts who walked our land talked about 'seeing with the inner eye'. This was a sensitivity to the creative forces around them – the wild wind blowing across the cattle fields, the barren rocked headlands, the brown-black riverbeds where salmon gathered, the hawthorn hedgerows or hearing the wild birds shrill song – all fashioned by the God who counted every hair on each head, who guided swallows home from African shores, who knew tears when life was hard and difficult, who watched children run through meadows when the harvest moon was sending the sun to rest. Such were the mysteries from the hands of the divine and loving God.

We can come to know the same God who continues to walk through history with us, because, in God, time is eternal and no day is ever too long and no night is ever too short. We can rise in the morning and *see*, or we can rise in the morning and *be*. We can become more aware of the God-given life that is emerging around us rather than merely rushing headlong in a day with all its frustrations and responsibilities. Such awareness does not come easily and will take time, but will offer a new depth to our living. Such awareness will draw us into a deeper place of peace and thankfulness and help us to become more centred and more restful within ourselves.

When we become attentive to what is going on around us, we are living in 'the now'. This is where real life takes place, and is really a microcosm of our whole lives and a good indicator of how life will be for us. However, we are so often fearful of looking and examining this space for fear of what we will see or come to know about ourselves. A well-known Indian mystic Krishnamurti once observed, 'We hardly ever listen to the sound of a dog's bark, or the cry of a child, or the laughter of a man as he passes by. We separate ourselves from everything, and then from this isolation look and listen to things.' So often we think that we listen and see what is going on around us but, in truth, we see and hear very little as we are so engrossed in

what we think is 'living'. Our insight is also influenced
by what we have known before, and it's usually out of
this place that we make our judgements.

When we live in 'the now', we have to be willing
to face the truth about ourselves and this holds the
key to self-awareness and allowing God to bless and
transform our lives. Many people are not aware that
when we live in the now with God, we cannot become
anxious and so the idea of a future without God can
only bring anxiety, just the same as being creatively
conscious of God brings freedom and its own healing.
It is in the present that we can and do experience the
'living' God. For those who want to develop a spiritual
life to embrace, this is essential. How do we embrace
the 'living' God? I remember once reading about a
traveller who went to visit a sacred, Shinto shrine in
Japan. Once day, the Shinto priest took him to a lake of
pure water. It was beautiful and crystal clear. Standing
by the lakeside, the priest asked the traveller to listen
in the silence and then asked him what he could hear.

'Nothing,' the traveller said, 'only the croaking of a
frog.'

'You have answered correctly,' said the priest. 'For
this frog will only live by waters that are crystal clear
and pure. You will never find him near stagnant water.
Only here will you find him.'

Our relationship with God is somewhat like this
in that when our lives are full of debris, clutter and
craziness, it is very difficult to find the 'living' God
because we don't have time or space to journey into
the quiet, the silence, into our very selves.

We should also not allow past hurts or anxieties to prevent us from being honest with ourselves and growing in self-awareness. The challenge will always be around the level of self-effacement we will allow. This may lead to a time of anger as we acknowledge our past hurts from, and disappointment in, other people. Traumas, such as sexual abuse or deep psychological hurts, may take years to overcome but in our ability and willingness to forgive and move on, we will find new hope and an awareness of God's living, healing presence, as I have experienced in my own life.

In his novel *My Argument with the Gestapo* the Trappist monk, Thomas Merton wrote:

If you want to identify me, ask me not where I live, or what I like to eat, or how I comb my hair, but ask me what I am living for, in detail, and ask me what I think is keeping me from living fully for the thing I want to live for.

It can be difficult to let go of placing importance on material things, but perhaps the secret lies in living with our hurts and disappointments in a new way. By bringing these things out of the shadows and acknowledging them, we give ourselves the freedom to begin a healing journey that may take a whole life – but at least in taking the first step we can look forward with a new perspective as we invite the God of compassion and sensitivity into our meeting place. Letting go of material possessions, adherence to selfish habits and busy, noisy lives to live a simpler, more natural, God-centred existence demands choices and decisions. Living a more simple life in which I deny myself of some of my great desires, also enables me to identify with those who have little, it enables me to share the burden of being without. When we can prune our lives, we can begin to appreciate small blessings more and we will begin to hear the inner voice of God who has been silenced by the noise of the world. As the Irish poet William Butler Yeats once remarked: 'We had fed the heart on fantasies, the heart's grown brutal by the fare.'

The voice of our creator may not always be clear, at times it will be like a deep yearning within us that we strain to hear. It is mysterious but will continue to call us, even now as you read this. Because we tend to live on the surface in many ways, we want to hear the voice of God in a similar fashion, but God's call to us is so much deeper, and is found only in the very depth of our being. To hear this voice, we need silence and stillness and simplicity. It is like going into the mountains to follow your echo. The more we call, the more we hear, but, the farther away our echo is. We strain and yearn to reach it, but never can. Yet, it is the beauty and thrill of the search that keeps us climbing. When we begin to search for and with God, our searching will cause us, as St Gregory of Nyssa, the fourth theologian, remarked 'to find God is to seek him incessantly'. The more we seek Him, the less interest the world holds for us. Then the night stars will seem more bright, the sun more warm, the rivers more life giving, the song of the bird more beautiful, the heart of another human being more tender and the presence of God more at hand.

Over the years I have witnessed great wealth but also great poverty. I have seen how those who are materially poor can also be very content and extremely gracious. I have also experienced the opposite among those who have power and many possessions. But a life that is surrounded with every material possession does not always ensure a life that is free from stress, suffering or challenge. More and more I am beginning to believe that simplicity is the key to appreciating the life that we have been given. To detach from much of what surrounds us , physically, materially, and emotionally, is a real challenge and one that I have to constantly make choices around. On my travels last year I had the opportunity to spend time in an Amish community in Ohio. For many years I had read about their way of life but was never near enough to explore their culture. Now spending some days in Ohio gave me an ideal opportunity and I was very fortunate when Kathy, with whom I was staying, provided me with a great introduction .

In Holmes County, which is near Dayton, Ohio, lives one of the great Amish communities, whose way of life hasn't changed in generations. These people live without the modern conveniences that we can take for granted. The Amish eschew the need for material things, instead placing utmost importance on family and friends, socialising in community groups and working together for the good of the whole communmity.

The morning I visit, the sunrise and the grey skies provide a fitting background to the rolling hills and brightly painted houses. Day comes early here and already signs of life are everywhere as paraffin lamps light the barns of the Yoder's Farm, where I am staying. My host has kindly offered to introduce me to this way of life, which has fascinated me for a long time. In the distance, more lamps illuminate the day and crying cattle walk towards the barn to play their part in Amish life. It is Saturday, the day before the day of rest, the day of the Lord, and already the natural cycle of life has dictated that work needs to be done.

Breakfast for my Amish friends consists of some warm oatmeal, followed by fried eggs with bread (but not toast) or what is known as an Amish casserole which consists of cheese, onions, some bacon and some hash brown potatoes, all gathered from the family farm. Apart from nourishment, food serves another very important function: it is central to the gathering ritual for families and friends on a daily basis. An Amish kitchen tells the story of Amish life and the principles that govern this way of life, a set of rules known as Ordnung, which is a German word that relates to rules, regulations and order.

This way of life is based on two religious pillars: the teaching of the New Testament and the regulations of the Amish Church. By applying the principles of the New Testament to the daily routine of life into this set of unwritten rules, the Amish Church regulates the private, public and ceremonial behaviour of the community. It is essentially a communal blueprint or collective wisdom that governs what is considered to be moral for the individual and necessary for the survival of the community. Walking up the country roads, I begin to discover that separation from the world is the key principle of the Amish way of life, which emphasises self-denial and humility. The outside world that I have come from is perceived to have been corrupted by vanity and vice, greed and violence. It's hard to argue with this outlook, but I am also left wondering about life within the community itself and how such moral codes are upheld – and if not, what of the consequences?

Though Kathy, my host, has offered to introduce me to the Amish way of life in so far as is possible, my inquisitive nature needs to be sensitive to these shy and somewhat distant people. A horse-drawn buggy comes towards me and a young man cleanly shaven passes in a slight hurry. Kathy reminds me that the young men will begin to wear a full beard only when they reach adulthood and are married, as having a beard is a symbol of life-commitment, as the marriage vows are taken very seriously. The young man who passes by, wears a broad-rimmed hat and is dressed in a blue suit with brown shoes. Normally I am immune to such dress codes, but in this incidence I observe his clothing. Amish clothing reflects the deepest convictions of the community's faith. The western concept of a person using clothing to accentuate their form would not exist among the Amish people. Clothes serve as a utilitarian purpose and should never be used to attract attention, especially attention that might be deemed sinful in any way or be competitive by making one person more attractive than another. Such a direct act would be harmful to the charisma of humility.

I step off the road as a young girl comes free-wheeling down the hill on what seems like a high Nelly bicycle. Her blue flowing skirt blows in the breeze and with a free hand she hangs on to a bonnet she is wearing. She is followed by two younger boys, also wearing bonnets, who laugh loudly and call after her. She is about fourteen years of age and I imagine that I have stepped back in time. They are completely immune to me, the *Englisher* – the name they give to someone who is an outsider and who does not conform to their way of living.

We reach the Yoder Farm and I marvel at the beauty of the wooden farmhouse nestling among the barns and outhouses with their distinct and clean lines, freshly painted in sand grey with white surround. Home-spun cotton curtains line the windows in a pale blue and flutter in the wind through an open window. I am an outsider gazing into a world that attracts me but also makes me fearful. Like most of the farmhouses in the district, there are sections built on and I am told that this is usually for the grandparents who will live and eat with the family but also maintain some independence by having their own quarters. I think of a old Japanese proverb I once heard, 'Happy the home wherein lies three generations.'

Nursing homes are unheard of in Amish life as they have no relevance in a culture that includes a *dawty haus*, a grandparents' home.

I feel like a tourist and yet I want to try and understand what sustains such a people and how they survive living alongside a tempting and secular world. Almost as if my company is reading my mind, and I am told about the tradition of *rumspringa*, which means to run around. On becoming an adult, each person is allowed to experience *rumspringa*, which is the 'English' way of life, or life of the outside world, before they commit to their Church and become baptised as full members, marry and settle down. Of course, I had to ask the burning question – what happens if the young person decides not to come back or wishes to marry a member of the Englishers? Herein lies the paradox for me. Such a person will become disinherited and must leave the family and community, never to be spoken of again. I understood how such an obligation would strengthen family bonds and ties, but I also realised how difficult and painful such a decision would be for a young couple who fell in love 'outside' the community. My friend tells me that most young people return to the community after their adventures in the English world and choose the Amish way of life.

The sun is rising and though the March winds are blowing cold, I see a group of men gathering and chattering loudly. Nearly all of them are bearded and wearing dungarees with wide-brimmed hats. They speak in hushed tones and rub down the horses nearby still attached to the buggies that have brought them here. 'They are building a communal barn,' my friend tells me. 'They believe that no one should have to work alone, so they share the work load.'

Immediately I think of the *meitheal* tradition of Ireland and my mind drifts to east Cork where my father grew up on a beautiful rural farm. Each August, all the neighbours would gather to share the harvesting of the wheat and barley and my aunt would feed the multitude with the best of home-cooked food and drink. As soon as their harvest was home and gathered, they moved to the next neighbour who looked after his guests in the same fashion. This was the heart of rural Irish life that knit communities and families in an unbreakable bond. After many decades, it was only disturbed by modern technology and the scourge of emigration.

My reminiscence is disturbed by a young girl coming out of the house carrying a basket of fresh bread. She passes timidly and the beautiful odour of fresh bread becomes very inviting. 'Amish cinnamon bread,' my guide tells me, 'otherwise known as Friendship bread. A very old tradition among the Amish and the recipe is a communal secret. Here come with me.'

We walk down Yoder Road and pass a line of laundry dancing to the March winds. I smile to myself at the order of clothes on the line, male and female, calico dresses and sensible trousers telling a tale of modesty and humble living. How out of place it would appear in an MTV world, and yet the simple beauty was eye catching. At the end of Yoder Road, we met a wooden sign reading simply 'Basic Farm and Home Store'.

'It's where you can buy the bread and other provisions,' my friend tells me.

Like a child in an Aladdin's Cave, I venture into

the shop of Abram Graber. Surrounded by breads, flour, biscuits, cheeses, washing powders, groceries, hardware materials, towels, home-made sweets, crafts of all kinds, religious carvings and wellington boots, I stand wide-eyed trying to take all in. The humming I hear comes from a generator keeping the coal lanterns burning, flickering light on the neatly packed shelves. The smell of fresh breads and cheese washes the room, and I yearn to eat some fresh cinnamon bread. There is no sign of neon, and beautiful wicker baskets are the comfort for eager shoppers. Behind an old wooden counter, two young girls are busy pricing items by hand and serving customers. An open doorway enables me to see another two young girls inside a back room preparing food for sale. They are engrossed in their task and oblivious to my stares – *another* Englisher is peering into their world. My inquisitive mind tells me that all the girls look the same. They wear blue cotton dresses, have white bonnets with their hair tied back in a bun. I try to make conversation with the girl who is at the counter, but she blushes and smiles at her companions. I am sure I am not the first – and won't be the last – who will evoke this reaction. We talk about the weather and I ask her about the cheese she is selling. She encourages me to buy some but when I tell her I have too far to travel she smiles and says, 'What a pity.'

There is so much I want to ask her, but I recoil. I have no right to intrude. A stern-faced man walks in and they speak. She smiles and returns to her work. We come from different worlds and yet our dreams

are somewhat similar. We long for simple lives lived in
a community that offers security, hospitality, empathy
and the certainty of God. One of us lives in a world
complicated by self-serving greed, insecurity and
angst, while the other lives in a world that will only
find meaning in order, humility and a life influenced
by a Christian ethos. The sound of laughing children
draws me outside. A young couple, have alighted
from a horse-drawn buggy with two young children.
They are dressed in the Amish style and the children
are textbook beautiful for eighteenth-century settlers.
They run towards a set of wooden swings beautifully
crafted in shaker style and call on their papa to push
them. The young mother peers from beneath her
bonnet smiling and encouraging her husband. I cannot
but think of my own brothers and their wives who
would react in the very same way. Two cultures, miles
and worlds apart, but sharing the same dream for their
children – a world of safety, fulfilment and security
and a visit from a God, who from time to time reveals
himself from the hidden places of human hearts.

I gather the bits and pieces I have bought in Yoder's
shop. As I leave, I notice the words of an old Shaker
hymn posted near the door:

T'is a gift to be simple, t'is a gift to be free
T'is a gift to come down to where we ought to be.

A TIME TO
WEEP, A TIME
TO LAUGH

Lord
There is a lake of tears
Replenished each night
With tears of mothers and their children
Who cry for a new world
Under your watching stars
A world ~
Without fear
Without darkness
Without evil

Replaced by
A world ~
Of equality
Of justice
Of inclusion

Would that it would come ~

Then somewhere in a dried up lake
Will be found
New shoots of evergreen trees
And its branches
Will form a garland

Of Peace.

I was very fortunate to have grown up to have an uncle who was a fine landscape artist. Richard, or Rich as we knew him, was my father's brother and spent his too short life capturing the beauty of east Cork and other such places on canvas. His seascapes of Ballycotton Harbour or Ballinwilling Strand brought the winter waves to life, but it was his ability to capture autumn in all its browns and reds that fascinated me as a young boy when I walked through his studio. I can still remember the scent of white spirits, or cobalt blue and burned sienna drying on the wet canvas coupled with the excitement of seeing a scene completed. I remember standing in awe at the forms that came to life under a soft bristle brush and how a few strokes could beautify a picture unfolding before me.

Watching my mother indulge her passion in her local art class as she painted beautiful scenes, being with my kind artist neighbours John and Lily, who have encouraged me to take a brush in my hand myself and express the wild fancies that overtake my mind from time to time, or feeling the joy of standing in a gallery and losing myself in the sheer elegance of a Yeats, Rothko or a Monet, have all brought my soul to a place of transcendence. These experiences have always stayed with me and have brought great comfort during stressful times.

If I ever have some spare time when I am travelling, I visit a local gallery and experience the beauty of expression and colour as seen through different eyes. One artist whose work I have come to greatly appreciate and admire is the Californian John August Swanson, a visual artist working primarily in the medium of serigraphy (silk-screen printing), as well as oil, water colour, acrylic, mixed media and etching. The son of a Mexican mother and a Swedish father, Swanson's art reflects the strong narrative influences of his cultural upbringing. His array of colour, vitality and energy depict scenes of community life and offer much optimism and hope, but it his depiction of religious and spiritual themes that really captured my imagination, like a form of music for the soul. He has covered many biblical themes in his work, with special reference to social justice. Over the years, I have come to know the artist and revere the contemplative nature of someone who can present his scenes so beautifully but yet so originally. One of the pictures that moved me deeply was entitled The Dream of Jacob.

In this work, Swanson presents to the viewer a biblical scene of angels ascending and descending a ladder beside a sleeping Jacob. The artist's printed colours, like layers of paint that have been carefully applied through glazing by reverent icon writers, reflect the artist's appreciation for his subject and his deep consideration of or fondness for his selected scene. The level of planning involved with registering multiple colours and co-ordinating the colour mix and placement so that they achieve a light-filled, jewel-like effect on the sheet seems to indicate that the artist wishes to present to the viewer a visual prayer. Swanson's ability to present a night sky that is almost translucent held me spellbound and drew me back to this work many times. His intense yellows and blues, artfully achieved, reach out from the painting to inspire the viewer and act as an instrument of contemplation. He is one of the few living artists whose work hangs in the Vatican Collection of Modern Religious Art.

I have always found conversation with Swanson to be stimulating and life giving, and recall his description of what art means to him:

> *Art is important as a way of communication to reach people. It goes beyond borders, beyond the rational. I'm trying to convey transcendent ideas that will empower people to take the next step on their journey.*

I remember him once saying that he had received 'many touching letters' from viewers of his work, especially from those suffering from illness. The family of one woman told him their loved one was clutching his illustrated book of St Francis when she died – a profound statement in itself!

His work also often includes images from the world of entertainment, especially the world of the circus. In one such painting, which is entitled Jester, he expresses his sense of wonder and his gift for 'finding the sacred in the ordinary'.

In this work, the clown-like figure rises from his sleep and climbs a ladder to gaze through a high window into an amazing star-studded night sky. To use Swanson's own words: 'The jester climbs the ladder to identify with the wonder of the universe.' But the scene is more richly complex than this.

In 1986, Swanson had completed the serigraph Dream of Jacob, with which I fell in love. In this work, the biblical figure of Jacob is lying asleep on the ground amidst lofty mountains. Starting not far from his head and extending high into the starry heavens is a glowing ladder on which many angels are ascending and descending.

As Swanson himself points out, there is a connection between the jester's ladder and the ladder of Jacob's dream. That makes sense. For are not clowns, dreamers, artists, mystics and people of imagination keenly attuned to the constant interaction between heaven and earth – the sacred and the ordinary, God and humankind?

Standing before his work became a prayer of

images for me. How often do I feel like the Jester, foolish andaccomplished and yet yearning to become something greater on one hand and, on the other, yearning to bring heaven to earth by reflecting the compassion of God in the world in which I live.

So often we lose sight of the 'ladder' that exists between heaven and earth, so many people do not believe that such a connection exists and consign such thoughts to the fanciful. Abba sang, 'I believe in angels,' – but do we really? Are they not just a figment of fantasy and imagination?

If we look to the Bible, we see that both the Old Testament and the New Testament have many examples of the presence of angels. The word 'angel' comes from the Greek 'aggelos' which means 'messenger'. The angels reveal the mystery and plan of God for his people. The New Testament includes many interactions and conversations between angels and humans. For instance, three separate cases of angelic interaction deal with the births of John the Baptist and Jesus Christ. In Luke 1:11, an angel appears to Zechariah to inform him that he will have a child despite his old age, thus proclaiming the birth of John the Baptist. And in Luke 1:26 the Archangel Gabriel visits the Virgin Mary in the Annunciation to foretell the birth of Jesus Christ. Angels then proclaim the birth of Jesus in the adoration of the shepherds in Luke 2:10. Angels also appear later in the New Testament, in Luke 22:43, when an angel comforts Jesus Christ during the Agony in the Garden. In Matthew 28:5, an angel speaks at the empty tomb, following the Resurrection of Jesus and the rolling back of the stone by angels. Hebrews 13:2 reminds the reader that they may 'entertain angels unaware'.

In his work *Angels Participate in the History of Salvation*, the late Pope John Paul II wrote:

> *The Church has professed throughout the centuries the truth about the existence of the angels as purely spiritual beings. Illuminated by the light that comes from Sacred Scripture.*
>
>> *"God at the beginning of time created from nothing both creatures together, the spiritual and the corporeal, that is, the angelic and the earthly, and thus he created human nature as having both, since it is made up of spirit and of body."*
>
> *Const. Dei Filius, DS 3002*
>
> *In other words, God created both realities from the very beginning the spiritual reality and the corporeal, the earthly world and the angelic world. He created all this at one and the same time with a view to the creation of man, constituted of spirit and matter and set, according to the biblical narrative, in the framework of a world already established according to his laws and already measured by time. The faith of the Church recognises not only the existence of the angels, but certain distinctive characteristics of their nature. Their purely spiritual being implies first of all their non-materiality and*

their immortality. The angels have no 'body' – even if, in particular circumstances, they reveal themselves under visible forms because of their mission for the good of people – therefore, they are not subject to the laws of corruptibility that are common to the material world. Referring to the condition of the angels, Jesus himself said that in the future life, those who are risen 'cannot die any more, because they are equal to the angels' (Luke 20:36).

As creatures of a spiritual nature, the angels are endowed with intellect and free will, like human beings, but in a degree superior to them, even if this is always finite because of the limit which is inherent in every creature. The angels are therefore personal beings and, as such, are also 'in the image and likeness' of God. Sacred Scripture also refers to the angels by using terms that are not only personal (like the proper names of Raphael, Gabriel, Michael) but also 'collective (like the titles seraphim, cherubim, thrones, powers, dominions, principalities), just as it distinguishes between angels and archangels. While bearing in mind the analogous and representative character of the language of the sacred text, we can deduce that these beings and persons are, as it were, grouped together in society. They are divided into orders and grades, corresponding to the measure of their perfection and to the tasks entrusted to them. The ancient authors and the liturgy itself speak also of the angelic choirs and the activities that are proper to the spirit in the pure state.

*Among the books of the New Testament, the Acts
of the Apostles especially shows us some facts that
bear witness to the solicitude of the angels for human
beings and for their salvation. Thus the angel of God
liberated the apostles from prison (cf. Acts 5:18–20)
and first of all Peter, when he was threatened with
death at the hands of Herod (cf. Acts 12:5–10).
He guided the activity of Peter with regard to the
centurion Cornelius, the first pagan to be converted
(Acts 10:3–8; 11:1–12), and analogously the activity
of the deacon Philip along the road from Jerusalem to
Gaza (Acts 8:26–29).*

*From these few facts, which we have cited as
examples, we understand how the Church could come
to the conviction that God has entrusted to the angels
a ministry in favor of human beings. Therefore, the
Church confesses her faith in the guardian angels,
venerating them in the liturgy with an appropriate
feast and recommending recourse to their protection
by frequent prayer, as in the invocation 'Angel of
God'. This prayer seems to draw on the treasure of
the beautiful words of St Basil: 'Every one of the
faithful has beside him an angel as tutor and pastor,
to lead him to life.'*

In Irish spirituality, there has always been great
reverence for angels. The word 'angel' in the Irish
language is derived from two words 'ain' and 'geal'
– the place of brightness. The belief that the angelic
spirits come from the place of light, which is heaven.

Angels are depicted in much of early Irish sacred art and appear in the writings of St Patrick when he refers to the angel of the nation. The early Irish Christians held a great reverence for spiritual things and believed that they were protected by the angels in all places and at all times. Many of the ancient prayers reveal a close relationship between heaven's helpful spirits and a believing people. There were no boundaries in the Celtic imagination and such messengers were present in all areas of life. As the author John O'Donohue has written:

> *Your angel can see your invisible world and knows where you have been imprisoned, where the lost and forsaken parts of your life are locked away … You could ask your angel to go to the places of nourishment to assuage your present hunger and thirst.*
> Eternal Echoes

It is difficult to find a place for angels in a modern world without straying in to the place of crass commercialism, which I believe has happened and is very contrary to the meaning and spirituality of the angels. Their first and most important duty is to give praise to God and when they are sent on a quest as we see so often in the New Testament they interact in a very direct way with us humans. Angels speak to us in the voice of conscience and guide us with protection and concern. They are not mediums or spiritual entertainers and the notion that we can call on them without reference to God seems absurd and disrespectful to me. Angels have a deep appreciation of being in God's presence. It is often said that young children and babies can see their angels and are often seen smiling. Such angels can also see beyond the limitations of human sight and are very conscious of the love and concern of God for the child. The mystics tell us that no two angels are alike, no two are equal. God's perfections are infinite, and the countless millions of angels reflect these perfections in a divinely marvellous way. No two men, no two women, are identical, but the difference between them is relatively slight, whereas the difference between two angels is vast, complete. Every angel is specifically different from the other as one species differs from another. All the millions of men and women who people the world, all those who have ever lived or ever will live are of one and the same species, but each angel is an individual species.

Many artists have tried to depict the angels over the centuries. One such artist was known as Fra Angelico. Born Guido de Pietro in about 1395, he was an early Renaissance artist from Italy and described as 'a rare and perfect talent'. But it was Michelangelo who recognised the beauty and sensitivity of Fra Angelico's portrayal of the angels: 'Angelico must have seen these angels in heaven; otherwise, he could never have painted them as he has done.' Fra Angelico spent his life depicting biblical scenes and never retouched or altered any of his work because he believed that all his paintings were as a result of divine inspiration and so should not be changed.

So what then is the purpose of the angels in the twenty-first century where the sacred and the secular often clash and where many are wandering desperately seeking for some meaning in life and hoping for something deeper? The angels exist to bring the hope and protection of God into our lives though we all have free will and can make choices of our own. Before God, they offer prayer and good works on our behalf. They protect us from harm and danger and perhaps we will never know how until the book of life is opened for us at the end of time. They often reveal the will of God to us, as we have seen so many times in the New Testament.

Perhaps unknowingly, we too have encountered the angels in our own lives in various guises and forms as they reveal to us the goodness and compassion of God, who longs to be close to us.

A few years back, in Dublin, I had a back injury, and took a trip to the pharmacy for anti-inflammatories. As I returned to my car, pondering the long flight to America that soon awaited me, I heard a voice saying. 'Excuse me, please.' I looked around and saw a young woman coming towards me in a hurry. I stopped and waited as she approached and asked me if I was Liam Lawton. I replied that I was and she said 'I really had to come and talk to you.'

She related to me a very sad story. Only a week before, she and her husband had buried their young son, who had died in his mother's arms, while awaiting a heart transplant. She described how she had come out this day to take some time by herself, away from home. She said: 'It is very difficult to let him go. I have been wondering where he is, if he is safe and well, and I long to know if he is being looked after.'

I could sense her deep loss and pain, and the challenge of having to trust that her beautiful little boy was truly in the arms of God.

'I used to play your song, "The Voice of an Angel", for my little boy,' she told me. Today, when I arrived here at this car park, I stopped and closed my eyes to talk with my son. I played your song in the car. And it was then that I saw you.'

I spoke with the lady for a few moments and then we went our separate ways. Her loss and grief were palpable, and I felt deeply for her. I was glad of this opportunity to make a connection with her, however small, and it reinforced in me that sense I've always held that there are no coincidences in the plan of God and that, even as we struggle through our own weakest moments, God can use our vulnerability and fragility to help another soul. I believe that we are surrounded by the guardians of Heaven who prompt us to hear the voice of God deep within, and offer us opportunities through unexpected connections put in our path to do just so.

A TIME
TO DANCE

I long to dance
With outstretched arms
Surrendering
To the music playing
Deep within the recesses of my soul
But my unsure footing
Stalls me
So often I stumble

Give me the courage to rise
To hear the distant drum
And dance to rhythms
Unheard before
With secure footing
Let me lead others
To move and sway
To the music of new wonder

Graced by your song
May the dance
Go on and on.

The rains had come! After eight long months of drought, the windswept sands of the Turkana Desert were muddied with a downpour that came unexpectedly in the night. I was sleeping in a galvanised shed, which offered shelter from the torrential rain, but made it sound like automatic gunfire on the thin roof. I huddled under a light sheet, eventually falling asleep with the tempo of thundering rain beating its own rhythm overhead.

To the traveller, Turkana can seem a hostile place. It is the northwestern most district in Kenya and is bordered by the Uganda to the west, South Sudan and Ethiopia to the north, and Lake Turkana to the east. It is the largest state in Kenya and its main town is Lodwar, from where we took the dusty road to Turkwel, for about an hour to reach our current resting place. The settlement's name is derived from the Turkana name for the river, 'tir-kol', which translates to a river that 'withstands the wilderness'. Living is difficult here. The way of life has hardly changed in generations as goats are herded and subsistence agriculture offers life and hope to the locals. However, despite the harshness of the beating sun and the immense poverty, there was a great warmth and welcome among the people. The children were beautifully shy, but like children anywhere in the world. Ollie, our host, offered my friends and myself a truly Irish welcome in the home he has made among these desert people, whom he has come to know and love and whose language he speaks.

After many hours travelling through the hot desert sands – the temperature is usually near forty degrees – exhaustion brought an early sleep as soon as sundown occurred, a welcome rest – or so I thought! Just as I settled down to rest, the heavens opened and brought the very welcome and wanted rains. About five thirty in the morning after a long night of turbulent rain, I woke up and for a semi-conscious moment I was unsure where I was. The rain had stopped and in its place came the drip, drip from a galvanised roof that had sheltered us well throughout the night. It was *then* that I heard it. Beautiful harmonic voices singing in a language that I could not understand. I presumed Ollie was up and beginning the day listening to his radio or CD player. Then, as consciousness became more real for me, I suddenly realised that he couldn't be listening to his radio or CD player, because he had no electricity! Where was the sound of music coming from? I rose and washed and went out across the yard, meeting Ollie on my way.

'Good morning, how did you sleep?' he asked

'Fine ...' I began.

Then he finished the sentence for me, '... until the rain came and went! I bet you are wondering where the singing is coming from at this early hour.'

'Yes. Where?' I asked.

'It's from the church,' he replied. 'When the people heard you were coming and that you were a musician, they wanted to prepare something special for you. So despite the fact that many of them became very wet last night because the rain penetrated their wattle huts, they came up here very early to rehearse so that they could sing for you.'

I was truly moved and walked with him across the compound to the sturdy but very simple church that stood at the edge of the village. Going inside, we were greeted by dozens of smiling faces without a hint of the discomfort of a wet night and, for some, wet clothes. Many were wearing very simple sandals made from old rubber tyres. There was the choir, along with some other locals who had come to join in the welcome and who ranged in age from nine to ninety. A middle-aged man, wearing a long kaftan, animated them. He was the local catechist. He bowed graciously towards us to begin the singing, accompanied by a solitary African drum. This was a memory that I wanted to freeze-frame. It was a performance of a lifetime without gimmicks, without cynicism, without any pretentiousness. It was truly beautiful. This group of people, who lacked much in material terms, sang in their own tongue in layers and layers of natural and spontaneous harmonies that I could only describe as a natural, God-given gift. Where or how could a people learn such harmonies if they had not been given a natural gift to be used and enjoyed with great generosity?

As they sang, they began to dance and invited us to join them. The hypnotic rhythms were addictive as they sang their hymns and songs to thank the Lord that the rains had come and that we were their guests at such a time. Their joy was infectious and compelling. Later, as I shared song in a language that they could not understand, I saw their eyes dance with wonder and awe that somehow the notes we shared could go to that place in all our hearts beyond our own limitations, the place where God dwells, the place where all songs begin.

The memory of Turkana will always stay with me. Time and time again, I realise the beauty and blessing of music as a language of expression when all others forms of communication fail. I have always believed that music is a divine art form and a gift from our creator to enhance our world. Music has the power to heal, calm, soothe or even anger the soul. It can draw tears or instil great joy and excitement, and it becomes a bridge to memory. I am often transported to other places and other worlds simply by listening to the work of great composers. I wonder how a piece of beautiful music is first created in the mind of a composer before it is filtered through his fingers to the pages of a manuscript.

I think of the motet *Spem in Alium* written around 1570 by the Renaissance composer Thomas Tallis. It was written for forty voices – eight choirs of five voices (soprano, alto, tenor, baritone and bass) – and is a musical setting of a sacred text. It is most likely that Tallis intended his singers to stand in a horseshoe shape. Beginning with a single voice from the first choir, with other voices joining in in imitation, each in turn falling silent as the music moved around the eight choirs. All forty voices enter simultaneously for a few bars, and then the pattern of the opening is reversed with the music passing from choir eight to choir one. There is another brief full section, after which the choirs sing in pairs, throwing the sound across the space between them. Finally all voices join for the culmination of the work. When I first heard it performed in the United States, I was overwhelmed by its beauty but also by the imagination that created such beautiful sounds, using a feather quill and parchment pages without any of the conveniences of modern technology. What a beautiful mind the composer had to create such exquisiteness.

Music is a very subjective topic and everyone will have their own pieces that speak to them in some way or another. Down through the centuries, there have always been gifted artists and composers who offer us new insights into the creative world – the divine imagination.

I could never imagine my life without music, and I am very grateful to my parents and my extended family who encouraged my brothers, sister and myself to continue to learn and perform. Had it not been for their enthusiasm, I doubt that I would be performing or composing today. I am often asked about the significant moments in my music career and there are some that are very sacred to me, but I am always very grateful when even one person in an audience is drawn closer to God, or if their lives are moved in some way or another, by my music. A composer of sacred music, or indeed any form of music, becomes a channel of God's gift and we can choose to acknowledge this or not. At various times over the years, there have been different pieces of music that I have heard or have performed that have become significant in my life's journey. I remember when I was struggling internally with what direction my life should take, the music of John Michael Talbot always brought me into a quiet reflective place especially his beautiful piece *Holy Is His Name*.

I was in Bosnia twice during the most recent Balkan's War. I went there first with a journalist friend who was doing some research. I was so shocked by the experience that I returned a few weeks later with aid that I had collected in the interim. What I experienced during those days I will take with me to the grave – I witnessed instances of brutality and shame of man's inhumanity to man.

I remember one evening delivering aid to a hospital

in a very dangerous part of the city of Mostar. When we got to the hospital, the only place that was in any way operational was the ground floor, as the other floors had been shelled. When we walked in, they were performing surgeries on the wounded without anaesthetic because there was none. We were taken down to the basement where many of the wounded were recovering and taking shelter. I saw many beautiful women and children staring helplessly with eyes that would have seen too much even if they were to live many lives. I remember being asked to sing some music and songs for them, and though I felt very uncomfortable and almost guilty for doing so, I realised that when we are able to forget about ourselves and use our gifts to bring healing and support, another energy takes over. As I sang and my friend Donncha played, I saw silent tears fall quietly and a quiet stillness settled over us despite the great turmoil all around us. As we left, a mother, holding a little boy whose head was bandaged, came towards us and said, 'Thank you for not forgetting about us.'

It was there that I learned the story of Vedran Smailović. At thirty-seven years of age, he had a bright future ahead of him as a principal cellist with the Sarajevo Opera, among other orchestras, then the war came and everything changed. On the 27 May at 4.00 p.m., a long queue gathered outside a bakery, one of the few that remained opened. In the line were mothers and children hoping to bring some bread home in a city that was falling apart and which had many hungry people. As they waited patiently, a mortar shell was dropped into the middle of them, killing twenty-two people instantly and seriously wounding scores of others. From his window nearby, Smailović saw the remnants and the rubble splattered across the pavement. It was then that he realised that he had had enough. He had had so many hopes and aspirations shattered in the grotesque depravity of war, something he had never dreamed would happen.

Enraged by the destruction and the tragic loss of innocent lives, he thought desperately about what he could do to help show compassion and solidarity. That night, he relived the horror in his dreams, haunted by the screams of women and children. He was not a politician or a soldier or a public representative. He was simply a musician. In acknowledging this fact, he found the true purpose of his angst. He *could* do something – he could do what he knew best. He could play his music!

The following evening at 4 p.m., the very time the shell had exploded, he dressed in his formal performance clothes (with coat-tails and black suit), and, taking his cello, he walked to the crater where the bomb had exploded. As bullets and mortar shells flew all around him, he played his music. As the shells fell and exploded, he convinced himself that it was merely the noise of his applauding audience!

Day after day, for twenty-two days, he returned to the same place and played – giving a song on each day for those who had been killed. He played his beautiful and haunting music, sitting on a battered camp stool amidst the dust and the despair. He played for the dignity of human life, for hope and for the dream of peace that exists even in the darkest of places. Asked by a journalist if he was crazy, he replied, 'You ask me if I am crazy for playing the cello, why do you not ask me if they are crazy for shelling Sarajevo?'

He continued to play his music throughout the city especially where the dead lay and in places of beauty that had been destroyed by mortars, and each day, he offered a 'musical prayer for peace'. As his story became known, he himself became the symbol for peace in Bosnia. The outside world learned of his story and through people like British composer David Philips, Smailović's message for peace began to touch lives. Philips composed a work for cello simply called *The Cellist of Sarajevo* in which he expressed all the emotion and despair in solidarity with his fellow musician. In 1994, the celebrated cellist Yo Yo Ma played this piece at the International Cello Festival in Manchester, England. The pianist Paul Sullivan described what happened:

When he had finished, Yo Yo Ma remained bent over his cello. His bow still rested on the strings. No one in the hall moved, not a sound was made for a long, long time. It was as though we had just witnessed that horrifying massacre ourselves. Finally, still in silence, Yo Yo slowly straightened in his chair, looked out across the audience and stretched out his hand towards us.

All eyes followed as he beckoned someone to come to the stage, and an indescribable electric shock swept over us as we realised who it was: Vedran Smailović – the cellist of Sarajevo himself! He rose from his seat and walked down the aisle as Yo Yo came off the stage and headed up the aisle to meet him. With arms flung wide, they met each other in a passionate embrace just inches from my seat. The drama was unbelievable, as everyone in the hall leaped to his or her feet in a chaotic emotional frenzy: clapping, weeping, shouting, embracing and cheering. It was deafening, overwhelming, a tidal wave of emotion.

And in the centre of it at stood these two men, still hugging, both crying freely. Yo Yo Ma, the suave, elegant prince of classical music worldwide, flawless in appearance and performance. And Vedran Smailović, who had just escaped from Sarajevo, dressed in a stained and tattered leather motorcycle suit with fringe on the arms. His wild long hair and huge moustache framed a face that looked old beyond his years, creased with pain and soaked with so many tears.

Since then, Vedran Smailović has settled in Belfast where he continues to perform and compose. His story is far bigger than he is, and its significance is only realised in the hearts of all those who dream of a better world – without hatred and revenge, a world of peace and harmony.

I have discovered in my life that music has the power to affect deeply our human condition and bring us closer to God who created this gift for us. The whole universe is a song, a festive chorus that celebrates the work of God and we have been invited to participate in this chorus. In the Catholic Church, we celebrate this in what we call the liturgy. We have the Liturgy of the Hours – the waking hours is the morning prayer, midday prayer, evening prayer, known as vespers, and then night prayer. The cycle of the day enables us to reflect, to pray, to intercede, to petition and to give thanks to God. We do this through song, silence and prayer. For me, silence is the sister of song, the place from where all our hopes and dreams, all our songs, comes.

As well as the daily cycle, we have the weekly cycle, which can also contain special days of recognition of the lives of special people, the saints, who reflected God's loving presence in our world. Such days are known as the 'feria'. The weeks fit into a liturgical year that, for us, is a symbol of the eternal feast that will never end. Within all of this, we add our own song, to the song of countless others, to the songs of the monks who chant day and night, but especially we add our song to the chorus of angels who sing in the presence of our Father who created all of us.

It is within this context that I have been writing and performing my music – which is my prayer, my offering and at times the only form of self-expression in which I feel adequate. At times, I love the silence, the birthplace of all song, but at other times I long to participate and be a part of a working and praying community which grounds me in everyday life, especially here in Graiguecullen where I live. It's especially in the brokenness of everyday life that I turn to music as a means of expression, as a form of prayer and especially as a language that can communicate when all other words fail. There have been many times I have been asked to preside at liturgical services or other such events where brokenness prevails where I have found much sustenance in song when words seemed trite and unnecessary.

In the aftermath of 9/11, I was very privileged to have one of my pieces, 'The Clouds Veil', become part of the repertoire for many grieving families and communities. Ten years later, the same piece has served as a connection as families and friends came to remember and reminisce. On the walls of Trinity church, which has become a focal point of prayer and remembrance beside Ground Zero, amidst all the photographs of lost loved ones pinned to the wall, there are also some lines from the piece:

And when the dark clouds veil the sky
God is by your side

I have heard countless stories from many families of those terrible days. I had known grief myself – I had written this song after the tragic death of my uncle who was a music mentor of mine and died in a road accident – but little did I think that my words could bring comfort to innumerable others. That a simple song written in a small schoolhouse could bring calm and comfort has never ceased to amaze me.

We never know how we can touch the lives of others even from a place of brokenness in our own lives. Music is the inner or universal language of God and so when we are in need of healing or when our spirits need nourishing, we can begin by learning to listen, deep within, to the song that resonates within us. Every song is born in silence but we need to journey into the silence so that we can hear properly. When this happens, I believe our consciousness is lifted and our world enlarged. Music quietens the heart and helps us to be more perceptive to God's presence or to be aware of the beauty of the world around us.

Perhaps I have been tempted to take for granted the gifts that God has given to bless my life. The freedom to sing and express myself is always very sacred to me and I am constantly thinking about the next piece I will write and where or how it will materialise. I am not someone who can just write for the sake of writing, I will always try and marry the lyrics with appropriate music. People constantly ask why or how did I write a particular song and my answer is almost always the same – I am inspired by interaction with other human beings and their life stories. Everyone carries their own unique story with all its brokenness and blessings. To be able to celebrate a life in song and words or to heal, move or inspire another through words and song is a very special privilege that I hope I will never take for granted.

Music enables us to move beyond our own limitations and can take us to a place of freedom and can open the doorway to beautiful possibilities. A couple of years ago, I received a letter from Peter, a man who is on death row in an African prison. The prison chaplain played a piece of my music one Sunday during the celebration of the Eucharist, and it moved this young prisoner. He wrote to me and to tell me how the music has touched his life. I felt humbled and wrote back, this time enclosing some new CDs. As I sent the parcel, I wondered if it would ever reach his cell – even writing the address had been distressing: Maximum Prison, Death Row Section. A few weeks later, the post arrived and included a letter from Zambia. The prison chaplain had written to me again, enclosing a letter from Peter. I sat and read the letter.

Greetings and prayers from Death Row! Today the prison chaplain told me that you had sent some CDs for me. When I received them, I felt my spirits rise visibly like mercury in a thermometer when you have a temperature. I ended up dancing and leaping around my cell! … Thank you for making music that brings an inner peace to us. I am touched by the words you say, that 'music is a link with the past, finding its inspiration in the songs of other days. But it also seeks to find a voice in the world that so often forgets the creator and the beautiful story of the Incarnation. Yes I agree with you as I realise that the world is wounded because of a lack of love and because it does not know who God is. I tell my fellow prisoners on death row that feel utterly unworthy that they can always approach God.

My cell is always silent and quiet, a different kind of silence when I can reflect and travel to places in my memory I was free and young without a care in world. Now I am like a caged animal and have been for many years waiting for my execution. All my youth has been swallowed up in this cell. Somehow, I am at peace. When I listen to different kinds music it brings a sense of calm.

I have always believed that music is a divine gift, entrusted to us by God to bless, heal, invigorate, calm and restore our world. It provides a language of expression that helps us find words for raw emotions, for joy and sorrow and all that happens in between but we need to truly listen in order to be moved deep within. Our world is so busy that we barely have time to stop, let alone listen. But if we are to realise the great gift that music is for us we need to learn to listen in silence, as then, being present to ourselves, we can begin to appreciate what is surrounding us in sound. My friend in prison learned to appreciate the beauty of sound albeit in a difficult and sad environment, but it enriched his life. When we become detached from our present circumstances through the power of music, we can enter a different world, a place where no other person or experience can touch us, like this. And we can return there again and again. This reveals a little of eternity to us – where music opens a gateway into the eternal presence of God – because where beauty is found, God is there.

A TIME
TO SEARCH

I have found You
Without warning
In places of surprise
In the gathering of thousands
In the face with open eyes
In the houses of the suffering
In the solitude of prayer
In bitter disappointments
In the blessings of each day
Though there have been glimpses
The quest will never cease
For when I think I've found you
You have taken quiet retreat
Inspiring new horizons
Infinity beyond
The paradise of promise
For You
My soul still longs.

A wise old hermit lived in the mountains and, once in a while, people climbed the steep slopes to seek his advice and wisdom – he was known to be a man of few words but rich in thought. His was a simple and frugal life, living from the natural surroundings and what they had to offer. One evening, he returned from fishing to find a robber upturning his cell. He watched from a distance, then approached the burglar.

'Can I help you?' he asked.

Startled to be caught, the burglar was lost for words and stood helplessly in the doorway with a few meagre belongings of the old man.

'Take it all,' the hermit said, 'but let me tell you that there is one thing you will never take from me.'

This made the robber curious, 'And what is that?' he said.

'Come with me,' said the hermit, 'and I will show you.'

The hermit took the robber by the arm to the water's edge and he pointed to the reflection of the moon shining on the water. A white disc of translucent light dancing across the water's edge. 'You can take all my belongings but never can you steal this beauty from me or my heart.'

The robber dropped the few belongings and walked away with his head bent low.

This is a story about values and priorities in life, but it's also a story of a journey, though the ending may not be as we might expect. We spend our whole lives searching for all kinds of things – peace, happiness, contentment, fulfilment, call it what you like. Some people go to the highest mountain peaks, others to the depths of the sea. Some people search in the business or IT worlds, others through sport and competition, some through the arts and the world of music. Sadly some also search in ways and places that are destructive and habitually damaging, though they may not realise it. Some people become paralysed in their search and can remain unfulfilled all their lives because they were unable to move in a different direction.

Ultimately I believe that we are innately searching for God, though we may not know it.

I know there are many who would scoff at this notion and and disagree, but I really believe that our whole life's journey is to find our way back to the God who created us – to where our ultimate home is – and that we will not find full peace within our lives until we discover our relationship with God.

Why do I believe this?

I think we need to take a closer look at the world we live in and the lives we live ourselves. The whole of creation is searching in all its many forms and languages. All humans, all animals, all forms of life seek the creator and cry out to God in their own way. Within us all is this great longing for love and acceptance, but we don't recognise it as a cry of love for God. We dress it up in all kinds of actions, some good and some bad. This is expressed beautifully in the psalm: 'Like the deer that yearns for running streams, so my soul is thirsting for you O God.'

God comes to quench our thirst in so many ways, but we are unable to recognise him because our image and expectations are so vastly different. 'How could God come to us in such a way?' we ask, when we see the crimson sky at sundown or the dew veiling the morning grass or the sound of a starling diving or the mighty waves crashing on the sea ledge or hear the crying of a tiny baby longing to be held? God would never speak to us in this way surely? In my book *The Hope Prayer*, I write about how I believe that God is forever writing love letters to us, but that we are so busy we hardly have time to see them let alone contemplate them. And yet they keep coming every day, endlessly faithful. And to ensure that we are not forgotten at night, He continues to search for us in a time of quiet contemplation. In the stillness, He shines diamonds in starlight and washes our gaze with a silver moon. All of these things reflect the goodness of a God who is beautiful and wants our world to be the same.

But He allows us to make the decision to find Him – the journey – and to accept His invitation. Only you and I can answer this call for ourselves. It is not always easy to say yes or to keep searching, especially when God hides from us when we need Him most.

There is a story recounted from the time of the Chinese invasion of Tibet, when the Dalai Lama was approached by a well-known *ripoche* (precious teacher). This man was very anxious about his safety, and so asked the Dalai Lama about whether he should stay or flee to nearby Dharamshala in India.

The Dalai Lama looked at him and replied, 'Well now, brother, everyone stands on his own two feet.'

This may seem like a cold-hearted response but it wasn't; it was an encouragement for the man to find his inner strength and to go forward in faith. In our own search for God, we too need to find our own feet. No one can stand in *my* shoes for me, it is a journey that only we ourselves can make.

We cannot search properly unless our minds and hearts know humility. This is where many people fail, because they go in search of God and fulfilment on their terms not His. I have met many people, some of whom are very successful, with wealth, status and popularity that we could only aspire to, who would never dream of going on their knees to acknowledge God, who humbly came among us as Jesus and who yearns for a relationship with us. It would not be the 'cool' thing to do, or it might be considered a sign of weakness. If you were to ask such people if they were good and generous, they would probably answer 'sure hope so', but it may be difficult for them to acknowledge any weakness or self-blame. Getting to a place where we can acknowledge God is probably the hardest journey we make, because when we eventually meet Him, we are called to be self-effacing and honest. After all, He knows our very thoughts even before we express them ourselves!

You may wonder why you should begin to search for God when you are happy with your lot and have settled into a way of life that you find fulfilling and this is a fair point. However, life is constantly evolving around us and all our relationships are called to grow and develop. I believe that God is constantly prompting us or, as I said, writing love letters to us to remind us of His presence but we don't always see. Perhaps some day we will and hopefully we will still have time to appreciate what comes our way.

If we truly want to find God, He will find us. If, like the Magi, we go in search of something wonderful, we may not find what we thought we would. The secret of finding God and where He abides, or even hides is found in a journey that takes us into silence – or as the mystics call it, solitude. This is where we truly hear the voice of God. But this journey will take time and courage. It will mean emptying ourselves, facing ourselves and eventually even letting go of the securities that we like to cling on to.

We need to find a time each day where we can try to be still in silence. Silence awakens in us a level of consciousness that we often miss because we live such busy lives. When we sit in silence, we take the first step to communicating with God – or to put it another way, we pray. When we are prepared to sit in silence, we begin to notice different levels at work. At first we are very conscious of what is going on around us, then eventually when we can let go of external intrusions, we become more aware of oursleves, our own thoughts and we try to quieten our minds and find calm. It can be so good to find peace and quiet in our crazy lives, so we are glad to find a quiet time. After this, we can become uneasy as we begin to remind ourselves of all that we *should* be doing or *have* to do.

Sitting in silence is a time when all our worries and woes can come to the surface and we want to switch off and run – especially when they keep coming at an alarming rate all rushing in to destroy our sense of peace! This is also a time where our hurts and resentments can surface, things that we would rather put in the background because they can be so disconcerting. This is a really important time in our prayer time, because if we can allow such experiences and memories to just pass before us without making judgements – rather seeing them for what they are and letting go of them while still maintaining our composure – then we will have achieved something important. It is the time that teaches us how to be humble but also the time that teaches us how to let go.

In the early years of Christianity, a man called Anthony decided to take Jesus' call to follow him very literally – 'Sell what you own and give to the poor and come follow me.' Anthony went to live in the Scetes Desert of Egypt and was followed by many young men and women who wanted to give their lives to Christ. They lived as hermits renouncing all the riches of life. In truth, they were the early fathers and mothers of the monasticism that has developed down through the centuries. The emphasis of the Desert Fathers and Mothers was to live the teachings of Christ and many of them developed a reputation for holiness and wisdom. After some time, people began to travel out to the desert in search of these people to seek their advice and wisdom. Some of their sayings have been gathered into a collection known as *The Sayings of the Desert Fathers*. They often recited and chanted their prayers and psalms aloud while doing manual labour described by one the Desert Fathers, John Cassian, as 'the ascent to deep mystical prayer and mystical contemplation'.

It is from such people that we can find direction and wisdom in our own search for God and inner peace. Though the centuries may divide us, we can draw strength and encouragement from Amma Syncletia, a Desert Mother who wrote in the fourth century:

In the beginning of prayer there is a struggle and lots of work for those who come near to God. But after that, there is indescribable joy. It is just like building a fire: at first it is smoky and your eyes water, but later you get the desired result. Thus we ought to light the divine fire in ourselves with tears and effort.

The decision to find this peace takes time and courage, because in searching for it, we will encounter memories that may sometimes hurt and haunt us. This is when our subconscious replays for us the experiences that lie buried within our past and come to surface when we are in silence. This is when we can learn to see things from a different perspective, to be less judgemental of ourselves and of others. This is the time where we allow ourselves to tell our stories in a more self-effacing and more honest way, when all our masks and barriers are removed and we see our naked selves. More importantly, it is when we can come to God without any pretensions, without any facades, without any pretences. And there is much freedom in this. God see us and loves us for exactly who we are. The more time we spend in God's company the more like Him we become, and the more we can identify with Him. Ernesto Cardinale expresses it beautifully when he says, 'Our destiny is to be a portrait – a self-portrait – of God.'

God has presented some people with a relationship that they may not have wanted but which they have maintained in spite of great troubles.

I first read about the six children from Medjugorje who claimed to have seen an apparition of and talked with the Mother of God, when I was finishing my time in the seminary in Maynooth in the mid-1980s. I found the account of their story more intriguing because they lived behind the Iron Curtain and were suffering persecution – along with the other pilgrims who had gathered on the mountain side – at the hands of the communist government for continuing to talk of what they had seen.

Since that time, much has been written about Medjugorje and, it has become the most visited place of pilgrimage for Catholics and non-Catholics in this twenty-first century. Hundreds of documented healings have been reported and countless thousands of people have had life-changing experiences in this little village set in the mountains near Mostar in Bosnia, the place where eastern and western cultures have met over the centuries in times of turmoil and times of peace.

This was all I knew when I set out to learn more of the story that was unfolding in this little hamlet in the Balkan Peninsula. I travelled by air into a small but very dangerous military airport just outside of Mostar – flying into this airport has since been discontinued because of its location between two mountains, which proved an area of high aviation risk. I travelled by coach the short distance of eighteen kilometres and soon found myself in the middle of a small valley with a twin-spired church and a number of houses surrounding it. Many people were congregated around the church. The multicoloured headscarves of old eastern European women covering weather-beaten, lined faces told a huge story in its own right, in a country where communism had wreaked havoc on Christian communities and where God had been consigned to a hidden underground Church. Soldiers and policemen were everywhere and walked with hostile glares. Already at the airport, I had been taken aside and strip-searched because my passport photograph declared me to be a priest. The food I brought for the family I would be staying with was taken from me, including a rich fruit-cake my mother had made as a gift for the woman of the house. Taking the food from me, a very sour-faced police woman pronounced, 'Do you not think we have food of our own here?' I have often wondered who enjoyed my mother's cake!

My lodging place for the next ten days was to be in a typical Bosnian home, it was simple and basic but with great hospitality. An aged couple, Boza and Svetan, lived in the house with Baba Eva, the old grandmother, who was the Bosnian equivalent of the Irish woman Peig Sayers. She sat all day by the front door in the coolest part of the house, her fingers winding constantly around worn Rosary beads. The black clothes she wore as a widow were in complete contrast to the beautiful smile that she wore every time I met her. Though she could not speak any English and I had very few words of Croatian, we had an understanding and our own way of communicating. It would take a full book to relay much of my experience in those days – confusion, exhilaration, peace, struggle and awe as my life became intertwined with that which I can only describe as a mystery. If Heaven was really communicating with these young people, then the world should know.

Every night when the last prayer had been said and pilgrims went in the half light to their respective houses to share bread and food, I noticed that many remained behind at the church, especially many eastern European pilgrims from Hungary, the Czech Republic and Romania. They did so because they had nowhere else to go. They couldn't afford to stay anywhere after paying bus and train fare and probably travelling for nights and days to reach their destination.

One night I was walking by the church and I went in to say a prayer. What I saw, in one way shocked me and in another way deeply moved me. All of the seats of this huge church were filled to capacity with pilgrims settling down to sleep for the night. Rather than leave the pilgrims out in the cold night air, the local Franciscan priests allowed them to sleep in the warmth of the church. Wooden benches were at least of some comfort. It was here that I met George, a young pilgrim in his twenties, who had travelled for days to come to Medjugorje. I was intrigued to see so many young people here, praying and searching with great sincerity. George had been a university student and had saved his money to come. Because he lived behind the Iron Curtain, he could only remain outside his country for a certain number of days or his visa would expire and he would be in serious difficulties with the law.

When we met, I heard him before I saw him. One

evening while sitting the shade of the trees, I heard the most beautiful music coming from inside the church. Drawn inside, I sat and listened to the sweet and beautiful violin playing, each note suspended and ascending like an innocent prayer. Each evening, George would play his violin and express the poignant pathos of his people through his music. At night, he too slept in the church. I wondered how many of the young people I know would do the same. I watched as the old Hungarian women shared and broke bread with George after he had finished playing. I approached him one evening and asked him if he was hungry. He told me he was and I invited him to join me at the house where I was staying, as I was certain that Boza would welcome George with kind hospitality, which she did gladly when I asked her if he could join us. When he had washed and eaten, he headed back down the road to play for his people and steal some sleep on a wooden bench.

Each day I passed by Baba Eva and she would kiss my hands. Her simple joy was profound and her sincerity unquestionable. One day, I had the courage to ask her some questions as her granddaughter Zora, who spoke some English came by.

'Baba Eva,' I said, 'have you ever seen the Gospa?'

She looked at me with beautiful piercing blue eyes and replied with a touch of indignation, 'Of course, I did, we all did.' And she began to smile and cry and look into the distance. 'She was beautiful. So beautiful.'

'Where did you see her?' I asked.

'On the hill,' she said, pointing to Mount Krizevac which overlooks the village.

Why would an eighty-year-old woman lie to me? She, and people like her, who had suffered so much at the hands of the communist regime would only be incurring more hardship and suffering by promulgating such news and yet, with great courage, she and the people of the village continued to be witnesses to what was happening there. Despite having very few material goods, the families continued to open their doors to pilgrims who were flooding into the village. The parish priest was arrested and imprisoned for over two years and yet the government, try as they might, could not quell the fervour of these people. I met many people who had suffered great persecution at the hands of the local authorities.

One night, I rose to go to the kitchen for some water. In the dark, I almost stumbled over Boza and Svetan, who were asleep on the kitchen floor. They had given me their bed. Embarrassed and deeply touched by their generosity, I returned to my room. Since Baba Eva was not able to walk very far and was confined to the chair in the porch, she could never go to the church or climb the mountains to pray with the rest of the villagers each week. I offered to celebrate Mass for her in the family home. The family was so grateful but then I realised that this could endanger them with the risk of facing imprisonment. All church gatherings were strictly prohibited outside of the church building and anyone who promoted such gatherings would face the strong arm of the law. With my offer to celebrate Mass, I placed the family in a difficult situation – they did not want to offend me and also had a great yearning to have Mass celebrated in their home for Baba Eva. The family had to decide if it was a safe thing to do.

That night, I celebrated Mass in the quiet confines of the family kitchen. The doors were locked and the windows closed. Upstairs, one of the neighbours kept watch for anyone who might come unexpectedly. Only the immediate family was present. I asked George, my musician friend, to come and play as I knew he could be trusted and would not be a source of danger to my family gathered here in the dusk light. As we prayed, I was reminded of the early Christians who gathered in secret for fear of reprisals and persecution. I thought of the men and women in Ireland who gathered at Mass rocks in the woods and glens of each parish during the penal days, when Catholics were forbidden from practising their faith or having public gatherings of any sort. But that was then. Here every word I said and prayed was done in quiet whispers so as not to arouse suspicion of neighbours – I was told that even the walls could have ears in such times.

I gazed on the faces before me. Eyes that had seen much suffering and shed many tears looked in tenderness as we shared the sacred scriptures. Hands now bent in prayer, worn and weary from the tobacco fields and long hours of harvesting, eking a living from barren, stony soil, held the Eucharist, enfolding it with great reverence – a new manger in open hands. This is where God hides, away from the maddening crowd. In the silence of another starry night, the crickets joined in chorus as quietly and with great pathos George played his violin. No words were needed – beauty heals an open heart. Baba Eva wept.

As we finished, the neighbour on the roof balcony gave the sign that all was clear and the windows and doors were opened again. I walked back to the church with George who, once again, slept on a wooden bench and rose long before morning to allow the local women to come and clean the church for a new day.

George had never seen the Gospa, but he always played for her. George had never seen the beautiful Bosnian sunsets each evening gently fading over the foothills. George had never seen the other pilgrims who hear his beautiful music, and who were so often stirred to tears by the plaintiff notes that emerged. George had never seen me, or Baba Eva, or any visionary because he had been born blind. Totally blind. Trusting completely in the providence of God and in the goodness of human kind, he travelled by train and bus and on foot for days on end to reach his final destination and to play for the Gospa.

I watched him disappear into the church and I knew that I would probably never see him again.

I came in search of knowledge but I returned with so much more. The God I am seeking is hidden and revealed in the most unexpected of places, for blessed are those who have not seen and yet believe.

A Time to Keep, a Time to Throw Away

Michelangelo
You cast in cold marble
Pieta
Sculpted sorrow in
Serene beauty
Frozen in time
Wounds of love
Peered through a glass screen ~

But love knows not
The binds of paralysis
In time or place
The tender gaze of
A silent mother, whose
Falling tears
Washing wounds
That harbour no revenge

Looking to the heavens
Crying 'why '
Such beauty has to die

For letting go
Is signed
In tears we cry and weep
No hurt will ever steal
The love our hearts would keep.

One of the many privileges of being able to perform before audiences is the vast spectrum of people that you meet on any given night. I have always found people to be gracious and welcoming but also very attuned to the lyrics as well as the music. I am always intrigued by how two people can hear the same song and yet interpret it or be moved by it in a different way.

The people I meet after a performance usually say that a line from a song or its story has enabled them to journey into a particular place of memory – some good and some not so good. I try to make my songs reflective of life and of our search for wholeness and healing as well, in addition to the sacred songs and songs that I write which are specifically for worship. I always pray that my work will be sincere and find meaning in peoples' lives.

In these few moments, people can be very trusting and open, and I hope that I always respect that sacred trust. At such times people, are also vulnerable. The powerful force of music can move and sometimes disturb the tranquil rest of our hearts and minds, so that, sometimes, painful thoughts and experiences can surface. I am also very conscious that the few moments that I have with people will never suffice for proper support and counselling, but hopefully such moments can begin a process of hope and healing for people who genuinely want to move on with their lives.

Each of us struggles at certain times, but there are also those for whom life has been particularly difficult and I am finding that more and more of these people are finding the courage to come forward and speak. Every day, the media shows us the trauma and hardship that exist in the world, but I also realise that it is not *only* the strangers I see on television or read about in newspapers who carry wounds – people all around me are wounded, as am I. Very often the people we love most, wound us the most, and though it is difficult to admit, we can feel very let down by them and find it difficult to transform such situations into positive experiences.

I have discovered in my own life that it is not only important to ask, 'How do I move on from here', but also, 'Do I really want to move on?' When we become paralysed, we can root ourselves in a place that eventually becomes comfortable and secure, but which stops us facing the consequences of our wounds so that we can cleanse them, heal them and move on. Such paralysis can, in time, lead to self-destruction as we begin to identify ourselves as always being 'the wounded one' and are content to stay where we are rather than do something to change our situation.

There are times when we will encounter traumatic events in our lives and we will need help and professional advice to enable us to move to a new place of vision. For example, I am very conscious of the many families that have been so traumatised by the suicide of a loved one. Nothing can be so difficult or painful, and at such times much love, understanding and support is needed for those left behind. I believe that much more needs to be done to understand why so many beautiful, talented people decide that suicide is their only option. I have seen families torn apart with grief and guilt after the suicide of a loved one, and yet no matter what words are spoken, or how much time passes, people find it very difficult to move on from this place of great pain and isolation. Jesus assures us that the loving embrace of our Father will heal all wounds, but how can I experience this when my world has fallen apart and my faith is wavering? How do I prevent myself from falling into, and remaining in, a place of darkness and isolation? And if God really loves us how can He allow such suffering to visit people's lives?

One of life's lessons for me has been that *everyone* suffers – no one is protected but some suffer more than others. We can feel so helpless as we watch another suffer and feel unable to help. Their suffering not only tests them but also those around them, and the things that they believe and hold sacred.

True, we can learn many lessons through suffering as it prunes our hearts and minds but for those who are suffering at the moment, words can seem so trite and empty.

We all face our problems and anxieties differently. Some people I know will be able to talk about what they are feeling, others shy away and will talk about everything except their difficulties. Others still can react in ways that are out of character, simply because fear has become their overriding emotion. Our minds and imaginations have so much power when it comes to situations beyond our control and, at times, we need help to enlighten us. We need to encounter the places of darkness and anxiety in our lives otherwise, our wounds will continue to gnaw and cause even greater suffering. This goes far beyond the wounds of physical illness.

Our world knows many different kinds of wounds. In the past few years, many people have felt the pain of emigration, lost their jobs (and so are facing huge financial burdens and debts), and sadly some have become dependent and addicted to all kinds of escapes to alleviate their problems. The natural reaction is to ignore the situation in the hope that it will go away. The sad reality is that it doesn't, and may only get worse.

Wounds in our lives can cripple us but can also become the vehicle by which new blessings enter our lives. From such situations we can learn much about our lives and ourselves, but, above all, we can learn compassion, which will take us into a whole different experience in life and in the lives of others. My own brokenness, physical or otherwise, offers me a very gracious invitation and opportunity to bring a greater understanding and acceptance to the brokenness of those around me.

Sometimes we can be so wounded that time alone is not enough and we need professional help – and often the courage to seek it – but accompanying this, I have found in my own life that turning to God enables me to entrust my hurt and fear to Him who is all wisdom, all compassion and all mercy. Very often, these are the qualities that we long for in order to move beyond our places of imprisonment and pain. When we are in a place of suffering, we are also in a place of deep isolation – the journey through cancer, the separation in a relationship, the loss of work, a financial problem, death through suicide or some other tragedy – all of these things and more, can lead us into a place of great loneliness where despair is a constant companion. This is where our empathy can offer much to someone who is suffering. Sometimes all we need do is to walk in silence with another. Words are not necessary, the shadow of another walking alongside us is all the reassurance we need that we are not alone.

I have often accompanied people on their way to bury loved ones. In Ireland, we have a tradition of walking from the house of the wake to the church or from the church to the cemetery. On these sad days, no words are needed. All that has been said is enough, but to walk shoulder-to-shoulder with those who are heartbroken is both a privilege and a grace, for one day we too shall walk in a similar place and will greatly appreciate the footfalls of those who walk with us.

In 2011, I was particularly inspired by an art exhibition that was held in a small hamlet called Discoed, in Wales, in the Church of St Michael. The area in general is home to a number of creative artists, one of whom, Charles MacCarthy, with the support of another local, decided to commission a series commemorating the Stations of the Cross that would be put on display during the season of Lent, with the local Anglican priest reading a meditation before two of the paintings each Thursday. The idea was that fourteen artists would create a work about one of the stations, their names being drawn from a hat to correspond with a particular station. There would be no funding, but the paintings would be sold at the end of the exhibition with a percentage of the sales going to the charity, Freedom from Torture.

The background to each of the pieces is fascinating as each artist interprets the station given to them, and it seems as if it was the artists themselves who were most affected by the work.

When I visited the exhibition, after reading the biographies of each artist, I realised that they were a very varied group, ranging in faith from Christian to atheist to Buddhist. There are many themes explored in the works, but there were two pieces in particular that I found especially striking.

The first, *Jesus is crucified* by Nicola Hopwood, was

executed in stained glass. Against a field of crimson glass, the tiny crucified Christ lies open-armed, covered by a foreboding sky and framed in royal blue. The red is stark, but beautiful and full of pathos. Unlike any other crucifixion scene that I have looked at, Jesus is alone without his two thief-companions, which gave a sense of great isolation and loneliness. The use of the colour red, for me, accentuated the passion of the forgiving Jesus but also served as a bleak reminder of the continuing suffering of humankind and the innocence of those who suffer at the hands of others. This work is a meditation in itself. Staring at this piece of art, I am acutely aware of the aloneness of Jesus, dying with arms outstretched, and yet from this terrible beauty great good emerges. His dying words of forgiveness are written into history forever, the redemption of the human soul through the love of a dying man. He did not become paralysed in hate and revenge. Cynicism and loathing were met with forgiveness and mercy. It's no wonder that the soldier on duty was moved to say, 'Truly this man is the son of God.'

The second piece that I was attracted to was titled *Jesus Promises His Kingdom to the Good Thief* by Julienne Braham. On the cross, the body of Jesus is almost contorted in turning around in His final moments of excruciating torture to welcome one of the thieves into Paradise with Him. There is a huge poignancy in the face of the brutalised Jesus, but the picture is full of hope and an antidote to the great despair Jesus had felt in the previous few hours. Behind the figure of Jesus on the cross, colour bursts forth and the light-breaking sky is showered with flying doves. From the dark oppressive wood of the cross fresh green shoots emerge. The blues and greens of the painting differ greatly from the passion red that we saw in Hopwood's piece.

But the context of the painting also captivated me. In 2007, the artist's twenty-five-year-old daughter, Lucy, was brutally murdered by a schizophrenic neighbour. The attack left two families, who had known each other for years, struggling to come to terms with the awful consequences of the actions of a young drug-taking student.

Every brush stroke, the choice of each colour, the painting of the eyes of Jesus looking in deep compassion from his twisted torso, the final moments when a work is complete and the artist stands back to see it in full perspective, must have deeply touched the wounds in Julienne Braham.

What intrigued me was that in the exhibition each of the fourteen artists drew their station from a hat so no one knew which station they would get. For Julienne Braham to draw the station where Jesus dies on the cross, forgives His executioner and invites the thief to accompany him into Paradise, was intensely challenging.

In an interview she said:

> [I have] previously avoided meditating on the
> Crucifixion, but having to paint it, I came to see

the resurrection through, and throughout, the pain
on the cross. Up to now, I have seen the crucifixion
and resurrection as two separate events. But now
I can meditate on the death of Christ with a new
perspective and a new hope, with the mind firmly
fixed on the promise of Heaven, rather like walking
through a dark corridor with eyes fixed on the well-
lit room ahead.'

Written in the catalogue of the exhibition are the words
of Matisse:

The Stations of the Cross are not a procession. This
work is the deepest drama of mankind. Faced with
this drama, the artist cannot remain a spectator. He
is obliged to take part in it.

We are never spectators in life. We are part of it, and at
times we are wounded by our own actions, as well as
those of others. But we also have within us the capacity
to move beyond the dark into the light by realising
that we can make choices. We may be surrounded
by weaknesses and may be vulnerable ourselves, but
when we try to accept what happens as part of life's
wounds, then we can try to integrate this into our story
and begin to find a new landscape. It is the compassion
and kindness that we receive from others that will
eventually lead us to the light, beyond the darkness of
present moments.

God is not some disinterested figure in the far-off

distance who only intervenes when He chooses. I truly believe that God is *ever* conscious of the wounds and blessings that touch our lives, every moment of every day.

> *Yet not one sparrow falls to the ground without your Father's consent. As for you, even the hairs of your head have all been counted. So do not be afraid; you are worth much more than many sparrows.*

Matthew 10:30–31

Sometimes in the midst of all that is going on in the world we wonder where God is, and yet there is a piece of scripture that offers me much comfort. It is the episode of the raising of Lazarus (John 11: 1–46). Here we read of the reaction of Jesus to the death of his close friend. Even though He is God and capable of raising Lazarus from the dead, Jesus is filled with pity and is deeply bereft. We read that as He spoke, He prayed, 'With a sigh that came from the heart', as He stood with Martha and Mary, and we are told that He was 'deeply troubled'. Then we read the shortest but, for me, the most powerful sentence in all of the gospel stories: 'Jesus wept.'

Jesus, the son of God, the Messiah was moved with compassion and pity and wept. We see how this affects the bystanders who begin to comment as they see how upset and moved Jesus is. Henri Nowen, the spiritual writer, in his book *Compassion* wrote:

When Jesus was moved to compassion, the source of
all life trembled, the ground of all love burst open,
and the abyss of God's immense, inexhaustible, and
unfathomable tenderness revealed itself.

I believe that the same God, the same Jesus, weeps for us
and especially for our children, for the world's poor, for
the world's lonely, in all places of quiet desperation and
aloneness, with all who know fear, worry and despair. I
dare to believe that Jesus has wept even for me.

In the gospels, we learn about the people who come
to Jesus for help and healing – the leper who cries out
to be cleansed, the woman caught in adultery, the
blind man who sat by the pool of Siloam, Zaccheus
who climbed the tree to get a glimpse of Jesus but who
carried his own issues – all of these people and so many
more sought the healing of Jesus and were met with
compassion and dignity. The grace of knowing that we
need God in our lives is a real gift, and one for which
I am truly grateful. It brings hope and healing but also
the responsibility to change our lives and reach out to
those whom we ourselves have hurt or are affected by
our actions and decisions.

There is a redemptive nature in suffering, but
sometimes it is far too painful and difficult to take this
on board, as suffering is not easy or satisfying.

When we look back on difficulties in our lives, time
can give us a different perspective and enable us to
appreciate the various sides of every story. Time can
also help us to appreciate the good that was done for

us by those who reached out to us in love and care. The real lesson is that we, in turn, can do the same for others.

Recently, I was part of a group of people who spoke at an End of Life seminar for people working in hospice care. It was very interesting and I was deeply impressed by the care and concern of those who worked in end-of-life ministries, offering quality and sensitive care to people who are terminally ill. I was asked to speak about the connection of music and its role in the care of the dying. My audience was both attentive and very welcoming and really understood the value of music as a language to support us when we are faced with very painful emotional situations.

As I stood in the conference room of the hospital, I realised that the last time I had been in that hospital was when I retrieved the body of my uncle who was tragically killed in a car crash a number of years ago. I will never forget the grief and sadness of those days. My mother's brother, who was full of life and music, was suddenly lifeless and gone. He was a great musician and had constantly encouraged me to perform. In fact, I was due to perform with him the week after he died. In my short few years in ministry, I had been called to other tragic circumstances but when it comes to our own families, we have a very different experience. I had held grieving hands and hearts, but now I knew what that despair and shock were really like. Having to stand at an altar and look down at your family grieving is very painful.

In the days that followed my uncle's death, I entered a difficult place. At family gatherings, my uncle had always encouraged us to play and sing, but I lost interest and couldn't find the will to compose. I felt as if I was walking in a dark tunnel. Within the space of a few months, I had celebrated three funerals within our family – it seemed unrelenting.

About six weeks after my uncle's funeral, I still had not begun to write again nor had I any inclination to do so. After class had ended one day, I picked up my post and found a letter and a sympathy card written to me by a kind lady who was in one of my choirs. The card included lines from an old Celtic Prayer, which reminded me that God was ever present, though sometimes He can seem distant, like the sun hidden at times behind a veil of cloud. I kept looking at the few lines and it slowly dawned on me that they expressed so beautifully how I was feeling – walking in a haze of grey. That night something stirred within me and I took a sheet of paper and began to write some words, which eventually became a piece that I titled 'The Cloud's Veil'. Much of the grief and sadness poured out through my pen as I wrote the words and music. Sometimes we have no idea how our own brokenness can become the catalyst to bring healing to others, even though we are in dark place ourselves.

When I was in America just after 9/11, I met many people affected by this terrible tragedy. One woman came to see me after a concert. She was living in Washington and her husband had been working in the Pentagon when the plane crashed into it. He could not be found in the rubble as the walls and roof had caved in. They searched for hours for survivors. She told me that she waited and waited in great anxiety. She prayed for hours, asking God to keep her husband company whether he was dead or alive. After seven hours, he was pulled alive from the debris. Though badly injured, he was still breathing and managed to survive. I was deeply moved by her graciousness and her trust in God. She told me of how she had listened to 'The Cloud's Veil as she prayed, and I was humbled that a piece of music written from a place of great brokenness in my own life could become the conduit of hope and healing for countless others whom I have never met nor will ever know in my life.

We never know when or how our brokenness can become a channel of healing for ourselves but also for others. I have met some amazing people in my life who have become a conduit of God's healing in circumstances that can seem very black and beyond hope – yet it's the broken people who understand exactly what suffering is. From this empathy, a new landscape emerges and we are challenged to see life in a new way. Our horizon is extended and we are able to share what may have been until now an inward journey with others. This is how and where hope is born. This is where real miracles happen. This is where God reveals Himself in the most unexpected times and the most unexpected places. Such situations have taught me that I should always be grateful for what I have received, because suffering can awaken within us gifts and hidden qualities that we would never otherwise have known. Such experiences draw these reserves from us and we grow as people.

Mary Craig is a British author whose book *Blessings* I have always kept close to me. It is a story about the triumph of the human spirit, but also about learning to walk beyond our own perceived limitations, where, in the school of suffering great, difficult but beautiful lessons are learned. When her second child, Paul, was born with a rare condition known as gargoylism, she faced huge challenges. This condition rendered her son physically and mentally impaired and in need of much care. Overwhelmed by the problems of caring for her son, who was too handicapped even to recognise her, she went into a place of deep despair and helplessness. One day, she found herself volunteering for a week's work at a home for disabled survivors of Nazi concentration camps. This was to be a place of great healing and learning for her. Here, she met people who were terribly disfigured and yet were full of love and light, which enabled her to find peace within herself and the strength to accept her own cross. Then when her fourth child was born with Down Syndrome, she learned how to cope with this second blow with the response:

Self-pity is a cancer which erodes not only our courage and our will to happiness but also our humanity and our capacity to love. It destroys us and it destroys the friends who love us and want to help.

Mary Craig learned to move beyond the place of blame and self-pity but her situation also called her into a place of new appreciation and a different landscape which is captured elegantly by John Harriott:

No outsider like myself is in a position to dictate where the limits of love lie, or to criticise those who find caring for the handicapped an impossible burden. But it is astonishing how often [these children] draw out from others, especially their parents, hidden reserves of patience and affection. How we treat them seems to be in some wise way our own and society's acid test. In them, as in the Child on Bethlehem, we see, uncamouflaged, the native value of humanity itself, helpless, vulnerable, possessing nothing. And they have much else to teach. They are fearless: they have no enemies. They are trusting: their world includes no villains. They are loving: they do not doubt themselves. They are the ghosts of our lost innocence. Nicky [Mary Craig's son] will never build a car or fly a aeroplane or balance a set of accounts. But he never stops producing joy and love wherever he goes. He is a year-round Christmas gift, however crumpled his wrapping.

There are broken pieces that need mending in all our lives. To some, this means despair; to others, it is an opportunity to strain towards a place of hope despite all the obstacles and barriers. But if there is room for God, then there is room for hope as self-sacrifice and compassion open our hearts to new frontiers and bring us beyond the dark of night towards the dawn of a new day.

A TIME
TO SHARE

Humble seeds
In humble soil
With weathered hands
That work and toil
Become the wheat
The leaf and vine
Your gift O God
In love divine
And at your table
Each a seat
Remove the dust
And wash the feet
To eat the bread
And drink the wine
To others be
The living sign ~
That Christ is risen
As he said
No longer walk
Among the dead
For He is here
Let all believe
That every place
Is Galilee.

It was late in the afternoon and I was walking through some Dublin back streets to reach the car park where I had left my car. I passed a skip filled with rubbish outside an old building, and, as I did, something in the skip caught my attention. In the midst of cardboard, old tins, plastic and all kinds rubbish was a beautiful Russian icon of the Blessed Virgin Mary. The colours were stunningly beautiful in reds, gold and orange and, as I stood, I wondered, how this beautiful picture had ended up in a skip. A woman came from the building, and mustering up all my courage and without seeming judgemental, I asked if I could have the icon as it was going to end up in a rubbish dump. 'Sure,' she said. 'Take it.' I brought the icon home and cleaned it with oil. It is not an original icon but a copy of a Russian icon of Mary the Mother holding Jesus, but it was beautifully reproduced and now has pride of place on my wall. The colours are striking and, though I would love to see the original, I was still deeply moved by the eyes of the Blessed Mother – deeply penetrative and full of pathos, they seem to follow me wherever I am in the room, reading my heart.

Ever since I can remember, I have a great attraction to, and interest in, *reading* icons. Though they are much more a part of the Orthodox spirituality, I believe they have much to teach us and are a great grace to enrich the lives of all Christians. The word 'icon' means 'image'. Icons deliberately avoid a realistic natural look, but symbolise the transfigured, resurrected body of Christ, Our Lady and the saints.

An icon, however, is not just a holy picture – it does not portray a physical, photographic reality – but a spiritual reality. 'Iconography' is the term given to the art of painting icons, which require a certain discipline and training. The painter undergoes extensive preparation, including a spiritual discipline. When he has received the blessing from the bishop to undertake the ministry, usually only after years of technical and spiritual training (icon painting cannot simply be a secular hobby with a religious theme), the iconographer receives the sacraments of confession and communion, and enters into a period of prayer and fasting, in which he asks for prayers of intercession from the saints he is about to portray. Even the paints, brushes and other materials to be used in painting the icon are customarily blessed before work begins. The painter will begin with a non-resinous wood (birch and linden are favourites), and traditionally a groove is cut across the back of the panel, and a strut inserted to prevent warping.

Painting or *reading* an icon represents a spiritual journey for the artist and this will be reflected in the technique he uses. Darker colours and tones are always applied first and paints are mixed with egg white to form a certain pigmentation. The darker colours are followed by lighter tones, concentrating the light to certain areas to achieve the effect of mystery and beauty that we see in the icons. Many original icons also contain gold leaf, especially for halos that depict the supernatural mystery of Jesus, Mary or the saints. Eventually, the icon is left to dry before being varnished to prevent the colours from fading. When it is complete, the icon is placed on the altar and blessed. This is not merely a ritual, but carries with it the prayers of great traditions, for soon many prayers will rise up to Heaven before it – the prayers of a pilgrim people in a pilgrim church. It will become a source of grace and blessing for all who will gaze on it.

There is a tradition that the first icon was made by Christ Himself. According to *The Ecclesiastical History of Evagrius*, a leper named Abgar had heard of the healing power of Christ and sent his ambassador Ananias to find Jesus and ask for His prayers. Because of the crowd, Ananias was not able to get close to the Lord, and had to content himself with sketching Him from a distance. Christ, realising the poor man's predicament, took a linen cloth, pressed it to His face, and gave it to Ananias, promising to send one of His disciples to

Edessa, where Evagrius and Abgar lived, after His Ascension. Disappointed, Ananias returned home and presented the linen to the king. The impression of Christ's face was clearly visible and the king was cured of his leprosy.

This shroud is referred to as 'the image made without hands'. When we pray the Stations of the Cross, we relate the story of Veronica who came from the crowd and wiped the face of the suffering Jesus on His way to Calvary. When she removed the towel the impression of Jesus' face had been imprinted. There is no known historical account of such a woman and yet her name comes from two words: 'vera' (true) and 'icon' (image). Thus we get the name Vera Icona – Veronica.

The images, symbols and colours depicted in icons are rich in meaning and represent far more than meets the human eye. Those who paint icons are called iconographers and must struggle not to express *themselves* but rather become completely transparent to God, and, through humility, become an instrument of God's revelation. Icons open up for us a window to Heaven and so each artist carries the responsibility of revealing God's loving presence through his or her work.

In my own prayer time, I have always found icons very helpful in reflecting on the mystery of God and his presence, as they carry with them so much tradition and prayer. In Greek and Russian Orthodox homes, families find a corner of a room to place their icons and turn to them at certain times for prayer, and lighting candles and votive lights. To a modern secular world, such ritual might seem feudal and old fashioned, but finding a place and space for God in our midst is at the very heart of all the gospels and our Christian belief.

Recently I received a gift of an icon for performing at the International Eucharistic Congress in Dublin. This congress drew tens of thousands of people to Dublin and culminated in a beautiful liturgy celebrated in Croke Park, our national stadium for Gaelic Games, at which I have also been privileged to perform my own compositions.

The icon I received is an Icon of Pentecost, the birth of the Church. It was during Pentecost that the disciples received the full measures of the Holy Spirit and were sent out by Christ to bring the gospel to all nations. When we celebrate the Eucharist, we too are sent to share the good news of Jesus Christ with others. Each time we gather as a community centred on the Eucharist, God lifts us up, cleanses our hearts, binds our wounds, then blesses us and sends us forward to share such blessings with others, especially those less fortunate than ourselves.

I am constantly asking myself how *I* can make this gift of God, Jesus his son, known to the world that I live in – a world that has seen my Church fall so much from grace, leaving many people deeply hurt, scarred and wounded. A world that has known much suffering in the past few years brought about by recession, poverty, war, abuses of all kinds and especially by a great isolation and loneliness that has led so many to take their own lives in quiet desperation. Is it still possible to find hope and healing in the present form of the institutions that exist today?

I am also constantly asked why I have decided to remain in ministry despite the great upheavals within the Church and in such times what sustains my faith. In truth, there have been many times in the past few years that I have struggled to answer this question but somehow I always keep coming back to the words of Peter to Jesus in St John's Gospel: 'To whom, Lord, shall we go? ... You have the words of eternal life.'

In truth, the one grace that has held me, especially in very difficult and painful times, is the gift of the Eucharist, the presence of the body of Christ in our midst. If I did not believe in this eternal presence, I would have lost hope in the institutional Church a long time ago. This mystery, this gift, this beautiful, humble presence of God is *so* undervalued and misunderstood in our world today, not just as a blessed sacrament but also in the challenge for us to be Christ to one another. Just as God gives Himself to us without condition, we too might give ourselves to our brothers and sisters who cry out day and night, for love, for consolation and, for hope. This for me is the *real presence* among us. It is the transforming power of God, who can reach us in the darkest places of our lives and open the windows of light, when we feel that all is lost.

I am always grateful to be a member of the community in which I live in Graigcullen, County Carlow, in the southeast of Ireland. To recognise the friendly faces of my neighbours, is to allow me to have a sense of belonging and a sense of security that provides a stable and welcoming environment to come home to. To know that there are people who care and are concerned is a real blessing in life that I treasure greatly.

But there is another community that has also been very life-giving for me. This is the community of faith that gathers around the table of the Eucharist to share the body of Christ. This is where I encounter the faith-filled people of God who encourage, heal, challenge, console and support me on my daily journey. This is the place where, together, we listen to the voice of God who tells us that we are beloved but who also calls us into a new place of hope and healing. The word 'Eucharist' itself means 'act of thanksgiving', and so all we do around the table is about gratitude.

To come together to celebrate the Eucharist is about bringing our total lives to God and before God in an act of gratitude – all our experiences, good and bad, all the beauty and brokenness, all the fragility and strengths are all there before God, but are all connected in this great mystery. When I stand with my friends, neighbours and community around the table of God, I am standing with and for all my brothers and sisters, the world over – in solidarity, in union, in sympathy, in empathy and in hope. It means that I accept the co-responsibility of sharing in the wounds of our world and that I stand ready to channel God's healing, forgiving love with and through others. Of course, this means that I need to examine my own life and reach the places of my own darkness, failures and brokenness, so that God can touch my own fragile life.

I believe that so many people today do not understand the full meaning of 'Eucharist'. On one hand, it can seem so ordinary; on the other, it is full of mystery and a most humble gesture by a loving God, for a people who, for the most part, have failed to grasp the incredible graciousness of this gift.

It is the story of how God desires to become close to us. It is the story of a great love affair between the creator and the created. The same God becomes one of us, who we can touch, hold, see, weep with, laugh with and dream with. He was born in the most humblest of ways in the most humblest of places, in Bethlehem (which means 'house of bread') and He offers himself to us in the most simple and ordinary way – in the form of bread. 'This is my body given up for you … this is my blood shared for you.' This is what we call communion, the union with Jesus, the son of God.

When we share in this meal, we become Bethlehem ourselves, the home of Jesus in a new way. Such a union with God is so intimate, mysterious and sacred that it is difficult to grasp the significance of it. God offers his Son to us, to touch, to eat, to take to ourselves. We cannot see and touch Him as the apostles did, but what we are offered is a very different reality – it is a union that reaches our deepest places, where God reaches us in our loneliness, in our fears, in our sorrow, in our doubts and especially in our desire to be close to Him.

In ancient Ireland, there was great respect for the

Eucharist and people went to great lengths to protect and reverence the presence of Jesus in the Eucharist. There are many beautiful prayers from the tradition that speak of the privilege of this sacred communion with God. One such prayer, 'A Íosa Mhilis', has been set to music beautifully and tells of the great privilege of one who is about to receive the Eucharist. 'Sweet Jesus my tongue is no seat for you, nor is my heart a proper home for you, pour your blessings on me and remain with me.'

In Ireland in the Penal Days of the late 17th and early 18th century, it was forbidden for the people to gather together to celebrate the Eucharist and there was a price on the head of anyone who convened such a gathering. Any priest who was captured was executed, as were those who harboured him. There was even a special reward – thirty pounds – for anyone who told the authorities where a priest was being hidden. Because of the dangers involved, the Eucharist, or Mass, was celebrated in hiding, often in desolate places – in woodlands and forests or in inaccessible caves by the sea shore. Often, rocks and other such surfaces became the altar and the places of prayer. As people gathered to pray, others would act as 'lookouts' to protect the men, women and children as they shared the Eucharist together in hiding. Many beautiful texts have been written of these tragic times and were often disguised in different forms and images to protect the people involved. One such piece is called 'An Raibh Túag an gCarraig' ('Were You at the Rock?') – the 'carraig' was the 'Mass rock' used as a meeting place and altar. The words appear as a love song:

> Were you at the Rock and did you see my Valentine?*(meaning either the priest or the host)*

It was a code addressed to a disguised priest or the people present, so the enemy would not grasp the true meaning, even if he spoke Irish. Death was also the penalty for those caught attending Mass.

> *Were You at the Rock?*
> *Or did you yourself see my love,*
> *Or did you see a brightness,*
> *the fairness and the beauty of the woman?*

> *Or did you see the apple,*
> *the sweetest and most fragrant blossom?*
> *Or did you see my Valentine?*
> *Is she being subdued as they are saying?*

> *O, I was at the rock*
> *And I myself saw your love*
> *O, I saw a brightness,*
> *the fairness and the beauty of the woman*

> *O, I did see the apple*
> *the sweetest and most fragrant blossom*
> *and I saw your Valentine*
> *she is not being subdued as they are saying.*

At first glance, 'An Raibh Tú ag an gCarraig' appears to be a series of questions and answers about a young woman, but in reality it contains a coded message:

I was at the Mass I saw the Virgin Mary.
I received communion, and said the rosary
I saw the chalice,
and saw the sacrifice of the Mass
And I practised the faith;
we are not being subdued as they are saying.

People went to great lengths to protect their faith at times risking their lives so that they could hand it down to their children and grandchildren, , so great was their love of God.

In contemporary times, there have also been many stories about people's desire to protect their faith in the face of adversity. In China a missionary I know visited a village deep within the mountains where the people had kept their faith despite great persecution. He was the first priest they had encountered in over ten years. Overjoyed to see him, they asked him to go with them that night on a journey. When darkness fell, they travelled into the heart of a forest in the countryside and stopped when they came to an old wall. All of the villagers fell down on their knees and one of them, with great reverence knelt and removed one of the stones from the wall. Behind the stone was a sacred Host – the blessed Sacrament – which had been placed there over ten years previously by the last priest to visit the village. My friend celebrated Mass with those people that night, and then replaced the Blessed Sacrament in the wall so that their prayer could continue. It was forbidden to practise the Catholic faith but people cherished the opportunity to have God in their midst.

But Eucharist is not just about God and myself in a personal relationship, it is this and much more. While I am fed and sustained from the Lord's table, I come to the realisation that I belong to the family of God. I also realise that within this family, many of my brothers and sisters are hungry and in need of help and nourishment. I am also aware that many of my brothers and sisters live in emotional destitution. If I can break bread within my own small circle, I must also break bread for the wider circle that knows great suffering and struggle. If I can recognise Jesus in the Blessed Sacrament, then I am called to recognise him in the faces of my brothers and sisters. Henri Nouwen the spiritual author once wrote:

> *Dear Lord*
> *If I cannot translate my faith in your presence under the appearance of bread and wine into action for the world, I am still an unbeliever. I pray therefore, Lord, deepen my faith in your Eucharistic presence and help me find ways to let this faith bear fruit in the lives of many.*

So many people of my own age and younger have left our Church, some with deep hurts, some with anger and some because of apathy. It is a real tragedy that so many talented and gifted people feel they have nothing to offer our Church today and that the Church has nothing to say or offer to their lives. It is a real sadness that so many people, especially women, have been so poorly treated and felt so undervalued and unappreciated. I often tell people that the reason I would like them to be part of our Church is because we are all poorer without them, and I really believe this. Change can only come from within. Very often we imagine that the Church is so perfect that many people who are broken, stained, struggling and searching do not feel part of the same Church. They feel unworthy and too imperfect to pray with us. This is a real tragedy. Jesus never excluded anyone no matter who or what they were. We, however, must realise that the Church is both the perfect Body of Jesus Christ but *also* the imperfect broken body of His followers constantly in need of healing, forgiveness and consolation. It is a place of inclusivity where *all* are welcome, and if people do not feel welcome, then we need to ask why.

In my own ministry, I find it edifying to celebrate the Eucharist within the community where everyone can participate – some sing and use their musical talents, some read and share the Word of God, some artistically create a beautiful environment for prayer, others serve at the altar in different capacities or are Ministers of the Eucharist, sharing the body and blood of Christ with the faithful who have gathered. I find it very natural and enriching that a mother or wife, who can bake, break and share bread at her kitchen table for her family and friends, can come to the table of the Lord and share the Eucharist with another family, the family of God, with neighbours, friends and even strangers. This is truly the body of Christ at work. The farmer who tills the field and provides the grain can share it with the community of believers who gather to celebrate the Lord's supper.

One of the other beautiful rituals, which has been within the Church since early Christian times, is the taking of the Eucharist to the sick and housebound and those who for whatever reason are unable to share in the community Eucharist. Members of the community bring the Holy Communion to them at the end of Mass, with the blessing of those who were present at the Mass. In the early days of the Church, St Justin Martyr in his description of Christian beliefs to the Emperor Antoninus Pius said that 'the deacons give Communion to each of those present and carry away the consecrated bread and wine and water for those unable to attend'. This is the origin of the tradition of bringing the Eucharist to those who are ill and housebound.

Home visitations give those who cannot come to a church the opportunity to receive the Lord and to worship Him in the company of family and friends. It also gives an opportunity for the family of those who are sick or housebound to come together and pray and share their faith and support. Some of the most meaningful liturgies that I have celebrated have been in this context, and have offered much consolation to individuals and families. We should never take for granted this gift given to us. It is offered in perfect humility by God to come close to us. Unfortunately, we live in a world that refuses to accept this mystery or has moved on and has become apathetic.

I have had the privilege of celebrating the Eucharist in all kinds of places and for all kinds of people, bringing the joys and sorrows, the expectations and disappointments, the dreams and hopes of people to the table of the Lord, sometimes in large cathedrals, sometimes in small churches, in hospitals, schools, by lakesides, graveyards, alone or in huge crowds. Each time, I have known and believed that God has been present in a special and unique way – in the people who gather, in the Word we share, and in the bread we break, calling us into a deeper loving communion with him and with one another.

Recently on my travels, I came across the now well-documented work of Dr Ricardo Castañón Gómez. A neurologist by profession, he had been contacted by the Cardinal of Buenos Aires to give some advice on a recent happening. At a Mass, a Eucharistic host had fallen on the floor during the distribution of Holy Communion. As the floor was dirty, the priest had decided that he would not place the host back into the ciborium – the vessel that contains the hosts – but instead placed it into a glass of water so that it might dissolve and then the water would be poured on to the flower garden to bring new life. About five days later, the priest went to the tabernacle and, on opening the door, found that the host in the glass of water had not dissolved, but that the glass was full of red stains. Over the next few days, these stains began to grow and were seen to solidify, defying all logic.

The cardinal thus invited Dr Castañón Gómez, a specialist and expert in his field, to examine the water and carry out some chemical research. The doctor visited the church a number of times and took away two samples of the water and stains for examination. One of the samples appeared in a gelatine-like substance and the other became like a dry scab of tissue. He then brought the samples to a laboratory in California but did *not* tell those there about their origin. The scientists in California presented the following findings:

The tissue was muscle tissue from a human heart
   The muscle was from the myocardium, the left ventricle.

These results confirmed what the scientists in Buenos Aires had said initially. Dr Castañón Gómez decided to take his research further by contacting Dr Frederick Zugibe, an expert cardiologist, pathologist and biochemist from New York whose detailed research into deciphering forms of death from anatomical information of the deceased is second to none. Dr Zugibe was also not forwarded any information about the origin of the tissue he had been asked to investigate. Having examined the samples, he stated:

The person with this heart must have been very
wounded. Under examination the tissue shows that
the heart would have been under great strain and
stress. The person to whom this heart belonged must
have been subjected to prolonged torture.

Dr Zugibe did not know he was talking about a sample
taken from a sacred host. He also said:

But there is something you need to explain. How is
it possible that while I was studying this sample, the
sample was moving, beating? So please explain how
did you remove the heart of a dead man and bring it
alive to me here in a lab in New York?

Dr Castañón Gómez relates the utter shock and
amazement of Dr Zugibe on being told of the origins
of this tissue of his research.

Dr Castañón Gómez was asked about his initial
research in Buenos Aires, and he refered to the notes
taken by one of his colleagues in the laboratory:

Some liquids are like red blood cells, white blood cells,
haemoglobin. But what I observe is that the cells are
still living, moving and beating. Usually after fifteen
minutes, blood cells die but after a number of days,
these blood cells are still alive.

Dr Castañón Gómez relates how he began to look
for similar happenings elsewhere in the world, and a
situation in the southern Italian town of Lanciano came

to his notice. This occurrence, also well documented, had happened in the eighth century in the parish church when the priest who was celebrating the Eucharist was filled with doubt and found it very difficult to accept that this was indeed the body and blood of Christ. When he looked down, the bread had formed into a different substance. In fact, five small particles of flesh had formed and though different in size, all had the same readings when weighed. Though this occurred in the eighth century, the particles remained visible and, in the 1970s, detailed research was carried out in the University of Bologna under the guidance of two scientists, both of whom stated that they were atheists. The following are the results of their findings on examination of the samples from Lanciano:

The flesh is real flesh. The blood is real blood.

The flesh and the blood belong to the human species.

The flesh consists of the muscular tissue of the heart.

In the flesh, we see present in section: the myocardium, the endocardium, the vagus nerve and also the left ventricle of the heart for the large thickness of the myocardium.

The flesh is a 'heart' complete in its essential structure.

The flesh and the blood have the same blood-type: AB (the blood type that the eminent Professor Baima Bollone uncovered in the Holy Shroud of Turin).

In the blood, there were found proteins in the same normal proportions (percentage wise) that are found in the sero-proteic make-up of the fresh normal blood.

In the blood, there were also found these minerals: chlorides, phosphorus, magnesium, potassium, sodium and calcium.

The preservation of the flesh and of the blood, which were left in their natural state for twelve centuries and exposed to the action of atmospheric and biological agents, remains an extraordinary phenomenon.

The flesh was made up of all the tissues found within the heart; a skilled surgeon even of today's standards could not create this. The blood is, even today, living – if water were added to bring it out of the coagulated form, it could be used in a transfusion.

Dr Castañón Gómez, who has pioneered the work in Buenos Aires, contacted the research team in Italy to compare scientific data and evidence to discover that research and results show that it is one and the *same* person in both situations though they were formed hundreds of years apart!

I find it very fitting and consoling that the Eucharist would appear under the guise of a human heart. It is at the heart of our Church, where Christ is found. The heart is the place of emotions, of decisions, of actions and the Eucharist is a call to love, a call to action, a call to participate in the body of Christ.

Blessed Teresa of Calcutta understood this very well. She believed in two kinds of *real presences* – with the eyes of faith she saw the living Christ in the form of bread and wine and she also saw the living Christ in the people she so tenderly cared for, especially those who were regarded as useless and nothing, the dying, the lepers, the abandoned, the unwanted. She reverenced the body of Christ especially in the broken humanity she witnessed around her. On a visit to Dublin, she once told me, 'If I meet Christ in the Eucharist, I will meet him in my brothers and sisters on the streets.' She understood that the Eucharist was not something private for individuals but is offered to us to build a community, to build the body of Christ, to give sight to the blind, to bind hearts that are broken, to offer life and hope.

And when our Eucharist concludes it is not the end but merely the beginning as we move from the church out into the world, from ourselves to community and begin to search for Christ in the faces of all those we meet and who are searching themselves, even though they may not yet know for whom. For when we are hungry, we come to the table and Jesus offers Himself to us and we eat. But then when we leave, we will meet Jesus again, though this time we may not recognise Him, for He will be the hungry one, the lonely one, the forgotten one, the aged one, the needy one, the suffering one. And somewhere deep within, we will hear Him say,"For I was hungry and you gave me something to eat, I was thirsty and you gave me something to drink, I was a stranger and you invited me in, I needed clothes and you clothed me, I was sick and you looked after me, I was in prison and you came to visit me.'

A TIME TO
BE SILENT

Light a candle
On the ledge of your heart
Pouring light
Into the room of meeting
For soon will come
Your guest
Who speaks in fertile silence ~
Where no word is needed
And all troubled thoughts
Are hushed
In the silent embrace of hearts
And though you have known Him for eternity
He comes to make all things
new.

Meister Eckhart, the great medieval philosopher and mystic, said, 'Nothing is so like God as silence.' Throughout the centuries, saints, prophets and mystics have searched for that quality of inner silence, where solitude becomes a place of listening and communing with God. Some have climbed mountains and lived in caves, others have taken to the deserts and other isolated places, and yet others have sought to live a life of solitude on lonely islands surrounded by calming or stormy waters. Today, most of us are not able to live in such extreme circumstances in order to hear God, but we still have a desire to find peace and an ability to hear the voice of God, despite all the contradictions and conflicts that we have within us. For some, however, finding this peace takes them on a voyage of self-discovery or calls them on a journey to become pilgrims of the world.

Such a journey of discovery will teach many things, but will also call us outside of ourselves beyond the limits of our comfort zones where we will encounter real challenges and opportunities for growth and development.

There have always been people who were willing to go beyond their known frontiers to discover new lands and new places. These people travelled for many different reasons, longing to learn more about the universe and the world they inhabited, longing to find new places to live, longing to enrich poor lives with what the *new world* had to offer. But, there were others who travelled *inwards*, on a voyage of self-discovery, to try and discover the world 'within' as once described by an ancient Irish traveller Celedabhaill who wrote in the tenth century:

> *Time for me to pass from the shelter of habitation,*
> *To journey as a pilgrim over the waves of the bold and splendid sea ...*
> *Time to deliberate how I may find the great Son of Mary ...*
> *Time to rest after we have reached the place wherein we may shed our tears.*

So we begin to discover the world of the pilgrim. The word itself derives from the Latin word 'peregrinus' – 'per' meaning 'through' and 'ager' meaning 'land' or 'field'. The pilgrim is one who ventures beyond his own space or land into unknown territories in search of completion or a fuller understanding of the world. The pilgrim steps 'out' of life to find a more 'meaningful' life, to deepen his spirituality and so identify that which is sacred for him and also for the community. The pilgrim is more than a sightseer. He is someone who travels in a sacred landscape to find what the Buddhists call 'enlightenment' or what the ancient Greeks termed 'metanoia' – a conversion or a change of heart that transforms a person and offers a whole new perspective on life and its meaning.

Most pilgrims, both in modern times and in the past, hope to reach a certain *place* on their journey. This place will be a physical place but also a place within, where new life, hope and transformation is offered. I often wonder in awe and amazement at the ability the ancient Irish monks had to find such places of beauty when they decided where to establish their settlements. The external landscape offers a tranquil peace and beauty that is so often longed for by the soul within and the pilgrim comes in search of both.

Central to the journey of any pilgrim is the notion of solitude and silence – to take time to be still and listen. A piece of writing that has always fascinated me is a classic called *The Way of the Pilgrim*. A Russian work, the manuscript first appeared in the monastery at Mount Athos in Greece in the nineteenth century and was first published in 1884. It tells the story of a poor man whose journey begins when he is deeply moved after hearing the words of St Paul to the Thessalonians to 'pray without ceasing'. He sets out on his life

journey to pray without ceasing. The opening lines of
the narrative are very moving:

> *By the grace of God I am a Christian man, by my*
> *actions a great sinner, and by calling a homeless*
> *wanderer of the humblest birth who roams from*
> *place to place. My worldly goods are a knapsack*
> *and some dried bread in it, and a Bible in my breast*
> *pocket. And that is all.*

His quest leads him to a 'staret', a spiritual father
whose words strike a chord with the pilgrim, despite
all the other advice he has read or heard:

> *Sit down in silence. Lower your head, shut your*
> *eyes, breathe out gently, and imagine yourself*
> *looking into your own heart. Carry your mind, that*
> *is your thoughts, from your head to your heart. As*
> *you breathe out say, 'Lord Jesus Christ, have mercy*
> *on me.' Say it moving your lips gently, or simply*
> *say it in your mind. Try to put all other thoughts*
> *aside. Be calm, be patient and repeat the process very*
> *frequently.*

And that is all.

At first the pilgrim recited the prayer 6,000 times a
day but, upon the staret's advice, he increased to 12,000
times a day a few weeks later. Soon the pilgrim found
the prayer at his lips and in his mind every waking
hour, as spontaneous and effortless as his breath itself.

To remain close to his spiritual guide, the pilgrim took work on a nearby farm but the staret died and, by the end of the summer, the pilgrim's work was done, so he decided to move on. 'I wandered about for a long time in different districts,' he wrote. Eventually, he was determined to go to Siberia because there, 'I should travel in greater silence.'

> I took to walking more by night and chose to spend my days reading the Philokalia, a literary collection of writings of the Greek-speaking Church fathers, sitting down under a tree in the forest … when I came to a village, I asked only for a bag of dried bread and a handful of salt. I filled my jar with water and soon set out for another sixty miles or so.

To the pilgrim, the Jesus prayer revealed the 'inner secret of the heart' and the 'knowledge of the speeches of all creatures'. While his writings taught him the mechanics of prayer and provided the theological framework, it is the wandering hermit life that brought the pilgrim the physical serenity and the detached independence of mind and heart to be open to a higher spiritual level. He realised how dependent on God's providence he was and that no matter what happened, nothing could separate him from God. Little by little, he revealed a little about his life, how his parents had died when he was young, and how he and his older brother were reared by his grandfather. His brother had caused much trouble and bitterness, causing the pilgrim to suffer physically and mentally, eking out barely a subsistence because of poverty. His wife died with fever and he had found himself alone and impoverished. He then began his journey. At the age of thirty-three, he decided to visit Jerusalem.

> *I do not know whether God will vouchsafe to let me go to Jerusalem. If it be His will when the time comes, my sinful bones may be laid to rest there.*

So ends the narrative. What would such a book say or offer to us in the twenty-first century? While many people might dismiss such writing as nostalgic sentimentality, I believe the prayer and the life of this wandering pilgrim offer a profound insight and a new approach to prayer and dialogue with God.

Modern pilgrims come from many different backgrounds, but the search continues and the curious still walk. The ancient pilgrim route of Santiago de Compostela in northern Spain sees thousands of people walking each year. Known as the Way of St James, or the Camino, pilgrims have walked this route for more than 1,000 years, starting in St Jean de Pied de Port and finishing in Santiago de Compostela, about 780 kilometres later. Many start out as tourists and end up becoming pilgrims as they learn to listen to the voice within as beautifully depicted in Martin Sheen's recent film *The Way*. Each year, the numbers walking this route increase – in 1985, 2,491 pilgrims walked the Way; in 2005 93,924 people walked it. Why the increase? What is it that calls people to take time from the humdrum of everyday life to search for peace and wisdom in the country lanes of northern Spain? Is it the same as that of people over 1,000 years ago? What inspires people today to walk such paths as the Camino?

Some people walk the route to be part of an ancient tradition. Others for faith reasons, to renew their faith or rediscover it. For some people, a journey like this is an opportunity to rediscover themselves and to rekindle a sense of wonder and awe in life. Others may do so because of life changing decisions. But central to any such path is the ability to journey in solitude and silence.

For all travellers, there is essentially both a physical journey and also what we call an interior journey. There is an old Jewish saying, 'Carefully observe the way your heart draws you and then choose that way with all your strength.' On this inner journey, we get in touch with our deepest selves and are open to the inner voice of God who calls us to a new place.

Those who set out on this journey have to do so with few provisions. It is a journey that depends much on Divine providence, that God will provide and that those who walk this path will learn to trust. When we have little to protect, we can be more open and aware of new opportunities and less concerned with protecting what we have. Setting out on the journey, we surrender our path to God, which is not an easy thing to do as we constantly need the security of what we know. In our first steps is an expectancy that our journey will take us somewhere but we are not sure where. There is an awareness of a mystery in our lives which is greater than ourselves but towards which we are drawn. So we communicate with God and ask him to lead and guide us.

At some stage we are confronted by who and what we are – this is a 'metanoia', a change of heart. The following is written in one of the ancient books of the early Irish monastic tradition, the *Book of Lismore*:

> *Going on pilgrimage without a change of heart brings little reward from God for it is by practising virtue and not by mere motion of the feet that we are brought to Heaven.*

Change of heart can be difficult, painful and slow and can be helped by various rituals – even the journey itself can be tiresome, and so can challenge the pilgrim to move beyond his normal expectations.

Though it might seem like an apparent contradiction, the lone pilgrim does not exist. We read in the *The Way of the Pilgrim* how dependent the pilgrim was on the people he encountered along the way. Very often when we least expect it, an encounter with another becomes a grace-filled moment. The God of holiness can be encountered in many different ways and guises far away from the shrines and sacred spaces even among strangers. How often has God revealed himself through others in acts of mercy and kindness, in words of encouragement or even a simple gesture of recognition? How often have we climbed holy mountains and received a helping arm or a word of support when we most needed it? Such encounters are grace-filled and bless our lives. We cannot live without people and yet there are times when we are called into solitude so that we can learn more about ourselves and learn to *hear* the voice of God who can only be heard in the silence, as Meister Eckhart reminds us.

Just as one of the greatest qualities of *real* friendship is the ability to be silent while in the company of someone we love, we also learn that when we can walk and live with ourselves in a loving, caring manner, we are closer to reaching a change of heart. Because in our solitude when we invite the Spirit of God into our emptiness, we can begin to let go of the things that prevent us from being kinder, more compassionate people. This is how we begin to find the sacred place within our lives. This is the place of transformation where we can disengage from the false illusions of modern living. In his book *The Way of the Heart*, Henri Nouwen, the great modern spiritual writer wrote:

> *Solitude is the place of the great struggle and the great encounter – the struggle against the compulsions of the false self and the encounter with the loving God who offers himself as the substance of new life … solitude is not a private therapeutic place. Rather, it is the place of conversion, the place where the old self dies and the new self is born, the place where the emergence of the new man and new woman occurs.*

Of course, we do not need to set out on the Camino to find solitude. We can fashion our own places of quiet and contemplation. For most, the issue is not so much finding the place but rather making the time and the choice to be quiet. One of the blessings of journeying on modern-day pilgrimages is the very different kinds of people you meet, most of whom are searching for a more meaningful existence, which has drawn them into the silence. The beautiful ancient Psalm 51 becomes the anthem of such a traveller:

A Pure heart create in me O God,
and renew a steadfast spirit within me.

On most pilgrim routes, various rituals are observed, such as climbing Croagh Patrick in Mayo, or Mount Križevac in Medjugorje in bare feet – I have seen the dried black blood on bare footed pilgrims as they have ascended and descended these places. On the Tóchar Phádraig, the pilgrim path to Croagh Patrick, pilgrims carry and exchange stones, expressing the burdens and weaknesses of life to be left behind.On St Patrick's Purgatory on Lough Derg, I put my shoes aside over the three days and walked on prayer beds invoking the God of forgiveness. The ways of other religions carry their own sacred rituals, which bring healing and growth, not just for the individual involved but also with positive repercussions for the whole community. When such ritual or liturgical expression is communal, great power and energy is harnessed which inevitably encourage a change of heart through solidarity and spiritual unity.

Such change of heart brings pilgrims to a new place, a new understanding of themselves and new willingness to change. The pilgrim has come to a place of surrender. The sixteenth-century Spanish mystic, John of the Cross, portrays this beautifully in *The Dark Night of the Soul*:

> *God takes your hand and guides you into the darkness as though you were blind, to an end and by a way which you know not nor could you ever hope to travel with the aid of your own eyes and feet, howsoever good you may be as a walker.*

Often pilgrims will want to leave some memento at the end of their journey. The coin or medal that's dropped in the Holy Well, the ancient rags or photographs left on trees and bushes, the candle at the Grotto, these are all remnants of those seeking and the searching. The stones heaped upon stones on wild mountains tell their own personal story for pilgrims who long for new light and a deeper meaning, but who must lay down the symbols of suffering and struggle and give offerings of supplication, entreaty and gratitude

For some, the road is long and arduous; for others the nights and days become one. Giving up seems inevitable and yet from somewhere comes a new inner strength and desire to continue. The spire of the Cathedral of St James, the summit of a holy mountain, the final days of fasting, the last few miles and steps, the inward yearning of the human soul to complete its task and to be renewed lies at the heart of all such journeys. The Welsh poet R. S. Thomas wrote:

> As has been said, the point of travelling is not
> to arrive but to return home
> laden with pollen you shall work up
> into honey the mind feeds on.

It is good that we celebrate. It is part of our psyche and an essential part of the journey. For out of the silence comes the song of thanksgiving. But it is a celebration not as an end within itself for the sake of merry-making, but rather to celebrate what God has done for us and with us. In doing so we celebrate the Resurrection as we become transformed and made new. The ancient shell that was worn by pilgrims who had walked the Camino was not just a reminder of a completed journey but it was also a reminder of a promise – the promise of a new life which offers new hope for a better future.

But such encounters and experiences are not limited to those who have the freedom and the prospect to take such time to search. The real pilgrim route is in fact a journey inwards which can be undertaken at any time and in any place. What is really necessary is the proper attitude and willingness to begin the journey. The road to Jerusalem, the ruins at Ephesus, the way to Croagh Patrick, the hillside of Medjugorje, the Grotto of Lourdes, all of these can be visited within the confines of our own hearts and minds because the same God awaits us there. As the writer of the *Book of Lismore*, wrote:

> *You will not find God in Rome, if you do not find Him at home.*

It is in the silence that all journeys are born and it is in silence that we hear the voice of God, directing, calling, guiding and encouraging. For the journey of life is our great pilgrimage where each day we discover new blessings, new opportunities and new hiding places of our loving God.

> *Let us concern ourselves with things divine, and as pilgrims ever sigh for and desire our homeland; for the end of the road is ever the object of the traveller's hopes and desires, and thus, since we are travellers and pilgrims in the world, let us ever ponder on the end of the road, that is our life, for the end of the road is our home.*
>
> St Columbanus, seventh-century Irish saint

For years, I have sought refuge, beauty and inspiration in Glendalough, the valley of the two lakes. Nestling in the mountains of Wicklow, this valley has been a sacred sanctuary since around the seventh century and the home of the servant of God, Kevin. He came from the royal line of the tribe of Dal-Mesincorb. His life is full of mystery, signs and wonders but for a struggling Christian like myself, the greatest miracle is the beauty of this place which has become sacred through the prayers, the penance and the pain of holy men and women and countless thousands of pilgrims who found the pathway that winds down through the valley into this quiet and peaceful place.

Kevin was many things, a hermit and mystic, and a great disciple of early Irish monastic spirituality. He had an artistic temperament with a great affinity to the world of nature and lived in a stone cell on the side of the lake, which left him exposed to all the elements of winter and the harsh mountain winds. As a poet and writer, he wrote his story in six books, three in Latin and three in Irish. How and why does a dreamer and a mystic find himself in such a beautiful place? These are the questions that have haunted me since I set foot in the valley almost thirty years ago. It has become my haven of inspiration and the birthplace of many of my songs.

Like the ancient pilgrims of old, I take the high road from Hollywood to reach the valley. Leaving the world behind me, I wonder how and why Kevin came to this place in the first days. It is said that he was guided by an angel and I can truly believe this as I gaze into this sacred place now littered with stone crosses, broken walls and glassless porticos. Every minute brings new light and new colour. The fading sun dances shadows on the heather hills and the sound of bees humming was surely music to the ears of monks centuries ago. Wild yellow furze ornaments most of the valley as intermittent gullies throw cascades of water tumbling down mossy verges.

Today, like every other day, I hope that I will meet no one I know and that I can be alone with my thoughts. Like the pilgrims on the Camino who were annoyed by the tourists, I sometimes find myself distracted by the huge crowds that walk the paths each day. I want them to know the real story of this hallowed place. Making the journey here, I sometimes feel that I am leaving the world behind and yet it's when I walk by the lakeside or through the hills that I realise the world is with me. It is possible, of course, to come and walk the pathways skirting the lakes and be totally conscious of the natural beauty of this place but also to be completely unaware of the sacredness of this holy ground. We can no longer hear the chanting of monks, or have the scent of sweet incense wafting on the night air, or see the flickering shadows of candlelight on the stone walls. We can no longer hear the clamour of pilgrims' feet crossing the streams to find a place at the cathedral for daily Eucharist or hear the noise of soup kitchens and all the sounds of usual monastic life that goes with it, but the prayers and supplications of such people remain part of the mystery and majesty of this place.

I walk the roads and head to the Glendalough Hermitage Centre, where my friends Geraldine, Catherine and Michelle offer great hospitality and welcome to anyone who wishes to come to the valley in search of solitude and renewal. Nestling among the trees are a series of beautiful hermitages where people can come to spend some days and nights in restful solitude. There is a liturgical life and spiritual direction offered if you want to join with the sisters, but it is first and foremost an opportunity to journey into a place of contemplation and rest surrounded by nature's garden and good people. So many people have been inspired to visit the valley, that it is inevitable that such places would offer such opportunities. The Friends of St Kevin, which has been initiated by my friends Geraldine, Michelle and Catherine, seek to re-awaken people to the spiritual beauty of this place and their actions reflect the hospitality and compassion so worthy of previous occupants of this sacred land.

I journey farther up the road behind the hermitages to the local parish church, nestled quietly among the fir trees. In the quite of the evening, I sit in this beautiful, simple church and gaze on the icon of St Kevin which lies above one of the side altars. Like all icons, this one conveys an inner message.

Sr Aloysious McVeigh RSM wrote an explanation of the icon that reflects many of the aspects of St Kevin's life – his prayerful and hermitical nature, his love of creation and his affinity with the natural environment as is reflected by a blackbird in his open hand and a fawn at his feet. In the icon, he is seen wearing a priestly stole over his monk's garb, which suggests his priestly role in the community. Along the borders of the icon, scenes from his life are depicted, which hold deep resonances for the people of the past. The symbols of the icon reflect the kind hospitality which so often marked Kevin's life. Many of the stories about his gracious giving are hidden within the icon, the hand of God guiding throughout.

It was before this icon that I prayed for inspiration one autumn evening a few years ago. I came down into the valley when winter was beginning to make her wild presence felt and the autumn colours that leave a beautiful canvas, were being blown with great force into the nearby streams and gullies. I had come for insight, inspiration and the wisdom that had been offered before to other seekers. I had received a major music commission from the Irish community in Chicago and I wanted very much to honour the richness and the beauty of the valley. It was time that I returned something to this place and offered to others what I had received in abundance over the years.

So began the journey of writing a work that I titled simply *Kevin of Glendalough*.

It would be a suite of music and story that would tell the tale of the humble and yet heavenly beginnings of this city of God. I would read, write, compose, sit in silence or, on some days, I would come and simply walk in the presence of those who walked before us, begging this saintly man to help me to reflect as he would like. I worked with Gary Fry, the wonderful contemporary musical arranger for the Chicago Symphony, who brought great beauty and life to the work and my script was beautifully edited by Mary Evers, also from Chicago. I longed to bring my listeners on a journey, both physical and interior, where one day or any day they could return again and again. From the opening cadences to the closing note, we would walk through the life of this saintly soul but somehow I desperately wanted to make it all numinous and tangible and not some fairytale from a bygone era.

I lived each piece and each day would turn in petition to the saint of valley. I wrote a dance piece called *To Waters and the Wild*. It was a celebration of the seamless relationship between the natural world and the community who lived in the valley.

I was still nurturing the work and walking the winding pathways in the woodlands and St Kevin's Way, hoping that I might hear the distant chants of bygone days or the words of holy men and women carried on the wind. The work was written and arranged for an orchestra, traditional Irish instruments, choir and soloists. I would be singing some of the solo work with some singers from the US. I had worked with the choir director Bill Fraher previously and he had a great love and respect for the Irish tradition, being director of music at Old St Patrick's Church in the heart of Chicago and the place of workshop for the Irish-American community in the city.

I continued to work and, as the strands were drawn together, I heard that the actor John Malkovich had agreed to narrate the piece for the performance. I've always admired his acting skills from a distance, but now that this same rich and sensitive voice was to narrate the text – it was a great honour and I hoped that it would be expressive enough for him.

Symphony Centre Chicago is a beautiful complex, located on South Michigan Avenue. It is the home to the Chicago Symphony Orchestra and the Chicago

Sinfonietta and had almost 1,600 seats. Walking out on stage gave me the impression of how well built it was and how few bad seats there were.

Colin Dunne had taken over the lead role in *Riverdance* but had now finished touring. He graciously agreed to dance for the show. I have huge respect for the way in which he took on board the suggestions and especially how we created a beautiful dance by reflecting on the text. The piece began with a freestyle dance with three different time changes before the symphony orchestra took up the music. He received a very deserved standing ovation.

The people of Chicago came to hear the story of a saintly man from *this* valley in Ireland. John Malkovich told the story with a great passion and enthralled the audience with his narrative – stories of a man of God, but also a man of his people, a poet, a hermit, a prophet who would lead many to find their soul. I watched the faces of thousands drawn by words and song into another world and a deep longing by many to rekindle the ancient faith of their ancestors. I was keenly aware of the presence of Mayor Richard Daley and his wife Maggie who had, themselves, lost a son named Kevin when he was a young boy. This night was in his honour.

When the final curtain call had come and the capacity crowd was leaving, I made my way to my dressing room grateful and with a small sense of pride – pride in all the people who had made this possible but also gratified that more people had come to learn of this beautiful place. There was a knock on my door and Mr Malkovich was standing there. 'I want to know more about this place and someday I want to walk in the footsteps of the one called Kevin or maybe one day we will tell this story in your own country.' Someday, I hope to do so! And then perhaps we will walk on the road to Laragh, visit Trinity Church and skim stones on the upper lake and hear the chanting of ancient monks that he so beautifully narrated.

In the icon in the Parish church, there is an angel. His presence is a recurring one in many of the stories of Kevin's life. Perhaps he will continue to be a recurring presence so that people like myself and the many who come seeking solitude in this sacred valley will continue to be guided by the angel of this saintly man Kevin where time and space are of no consequence as we enter God's eternal time and the light that pours through the mountains and reflects like crystal on the upper and lower lake will always light the way for the pilgrim.

> *Cast away the dew of night*
> *And gaze into the lake of light*
> *Find the road where secrets lie*
> *Of Heaven's home in days gone by*
> *Where echoes sing of chanted prayers*
> *And broken stones sign hermit's ways*
> *Where weathered trees*
> *Their memories hold,*
> *Of pilgrims' lives, their stories told*
> *Where holy men once carved in rock*
> *The sacred place of Glendalough*

A TIME
TO SPEAK

Where there is beauty
Let me sing
Where there is goodness
Let me praise
Where there is wisdom
Let me listen
Where there is courage
Let me affirm
Where there is wonder
Let me be humble
Where there is loneliness
Let me be present
Where there is suffering
Let me weep
Where there is injustice
Let me cry out
Where there is condemnation
Let me bring integrity
Where there is deafening silence ~
Let me speak.

Like all professions, an ordained priest has to face difficult situations for the first time. As a young recruit, you have to learn how to respond to the circumstances and hope that how and why you respond will be acceptable and done well. Having had an academic preparation with little or no pastoral activity, I was appointed to a busy urban parish with a number of schools, a cathedral and a number of nursing homes. The town also had a psychiatric hospital that acted as the hospital for the county as well as the town itself.

One evening not long after my appointment to the area, I got an emergency call to one of the secure wards in the hospital. I was on my own in the house when the call came through and so with little or no knowledge of where I was going, I rushed to the hospital to assist the seriously ill patient. To say that I was nervous would be an understatement. With each corridor, another door was opened and locked behind me until, eventually, I reached the room where the man lay in bed. At this stage, my heart was palpitating and I was extremely uncomfortable, mainly because I did not know where I was going. Suddenly, I found myself in a room with an elderly gentleman who, though weak, was very gentle and helpless. I felt so ashamed for being nervous. I knelt beside him and held his hand and prayed sincerely for his healing and comfort. The staff were extremely kind and welcoming, but I had faced my own fears and preconceived notions on this, my very first emergency call.

I learned much on that day, but I was to learn much more over the years that followed on my trips to the same hospital. There, I saw the vulnerability of the human soul and there I learned about loneliness – the loneliness of entering into a world of depression, mental illness and the isolation that is part of such fragility. I came to know the patients not as strangers awaiting treatment, but as human beings with needs, minds and hearts as beautiful as the rest of us.

Thankfully, our outlook on mental illness and disability is changing but, in the past, many people were placed in hospitals and homes simply because they were different or because their families could not cope with their fragility or even the sense of shame at having someone belonging to them who was not the same as everyone else.

Such people became institutionalised. Some were simply abandoned and left in hospitals to be cared for by strangers who could never give them the same security that would be found in a home even though they were, and continue to be, some very kind and caring people within the health system. Many people who became patients of such hospitals suffered from deep sadness and a sense of rejection. Such pain can linger for life and be the source of extreme loneliness. It can cause people to fall into a sense of utter despair as they wonder what value they can offer to society. Sometimes this loneliness is manifested in a screaming or a constant agitation. Sometimes it can be manifested in a clenched fist or a body curling into a foetal position and not wanting to come out and communicate. Sometimes it is manifested in complete silence, where no one can reach the place of isolation and seclusion. The desire to live becomes less and less and the excitement of living ceases. I knew a young, severely disabled man, who was so closed up in his own life that he spoke to himself all day and ignored everyone around him. This was his way of coping. So many times I have wished that I had the power of the healing Jesus to free such people from the pain of isolation and depression.

I have no doubt that anger which has been turned inward has helped to continue the cycle of depression in sufferers. Mental illness is one of the last conditions that still holds a certain stigma and so engrains the isolation of the sufferer. It is no wonder that people in such a condition will do anything to try and kill the pain and get some respite from the terrible loneliness and remoteness that they feel, living in a world apart. So many people will tell you that they are unable to sleep because of anxiety and anguish, which leads to a place of confusion and segregation. I remember reaching out to hold the hand of a woman who was suffering desperately and being pushed away because she was afraid to allow someone close to her, because she believed she was not loveable. Feeling so unimportant and unwanted is a slow and inevitable death of all that is good and healthy.

Thankfully within society, there is a much greater understanding of the need for integration and a holistic approach to mental health, but we still have a long way to go to accept this condition without stigma and shame.

Many people experience some form of loneliness at some stage in life, but in dealing with it can become stronger and more intuitive. But there are some who are not so fortunate and can not embrace change and disorder when it visits, either unexpectedly or slowly over a period of time.Loneliness can come at any time – when we lose friends and loved ones, when we have to change work, when we become ill, when our children leave home, when we grow old. At such times, loneliness can overwhelm us and destabilise our future. Some people will try and to cover it to hide their pain, but one day they will have to come face to face with it again.

I recently met a man who had lost his son through suicide and who took refuge in a bottle of wine each day. He was so utterly grief stricken that he tried to numb the pain of being separated from the son he adored and loved with alcohol. Such scenes are all too familiar in modern-life. When the sad reality of the orphanages of Romania were discovered in the nineties, the world was shocked by the images of beautiful children tied to cots for hours each day with little or no human contact. Many of them stared listlessly and in silence, having lost the desire and the will to cry, simply because they realised that to cry out was to cry out in hope – but what hope was there that their cry would be heard? To cry out would be to use too much energy for nothing. When we, who are made to love, are never held or embraced in love, we can lose the will to exist and slowly and surely slip into a place of great sadness and aloneness.

There is within all of us a deep need to belong, to be loved and to be accepted. When this does not happen, we experience the sadness of loneliness and all that follows, which can be very painful. The inner child within all of us needs to be held and nurtured from time to time, for such is the way to bring healing and wholeness to our damaged world and damaged hearts. Very often people who are desperately lonely have a great sense of failure and low self-worth and it is when we reveal our belief in them that we can begin to bring healing to their lives. There is an inner beauty in each human being, but it is not always expressed and so many people go through life without knowing how much they are valued and loved.

I used to visit an old man who lived in the countryside. He lived an eccentric life and had few, if any, friends or human contact except when something was needed. One of his neighbours became worried about him and suggested that I call to see him. The first day I went, I had to climb over a wall to get into his house. Our first conversation was through the front door. He told me that he didn't need me to visit, but that I was welcome if I wanted to. So began my relationship with him until, eventually, he allowed me into the house. I was very shocked by what I saw. The conditions were dreadful, with no running water and no electricity. He had an open fire and on it there was a kettle (with no handle) boiling. I offered to bring the social services to help him but he refused, I offered different types of help but he always refused and I had to sadly accept his wishes. I also asked him if I could bring Holy Communion to him each week and he agreed to this. It was difficult to see in the dark but one day while praying, I saw a small statue of St Martin de Porres on the mantelpiece.

St Martin de Porres was born in the sixteenth-century, the son of a black slave and a Spanish nobleman, and he had an extraordinary compassion for the poor and destitute of Lima in Peru. Many people in Ireland and beyond have a great devotion to this saint. I began to pray through his intercession to protect my friend until I returned the following week. Over the months, the man's condition weakened but, still, he would not accept my help. I remember waking one very cold day, when the frost had fallen heavily, and not being able to appreciate the beauty of the winter landscape because I was thinking of my old friend in his cottage. I went out especially that morning to bring some blankets but, again, he refused to accept them, so again I prayed to St Martin to take care of him.

A few weeks later, I decided to call to see him midweek and I found him in a very weak condition. He collapsed trying to open the door to me and was on the floor. Eventually, with the help of a doctor and medical staff, he was taken to the hospital. That night from the intensive care ward, the medical staff told me that he was seriously ill and very weak. I was relieved that he had been brought to hospital to be cared for, but concerned that he might not survive. After a week or so in intensive care, he was moved to another ward and eventually to a nursing home in his own town.

On Christmas day, when I had finished my parish duties and was on my way to join my family in the midlands, I called by the nursing home to see my friend. I walked up and down the ward looking for him and eventually returned to the nursing station. I told the nurse that he wasn't in the ward. She looked puzzled at me and said, 'Well, he was there a few moments ago.'

She walked with me to the same ward. There, in the corner bed was my old friend. I did not recognise him. He wore a beautiful smile and had a silver-white head of hair that I had never seen. He was surrounded by warmth and care, and looked so comfortable in his bed of white linen sheets. Beside him on his bedside locker was a small bottle of whiskey, a Christmas gift from the staff. Three weeks later, unexpectedly, he died in his sleep. He had lived that latter part of his life in dreadful conditions but died like an angel.

Sometimes, loneliness and isolation can call us into a place where no one can reach us easily. We want to turn away from the world and hide ourselves. This happens when we feel that we have nothing worthwhile to contribute, when we believe that there is little value in our presence. Nothing could be farther from the truth. In the eyes of God, every one of us has a reason to exist and has something unique with which to bless our world. We are all broken, some more so than others, but when we feel appreciated and accepted we can learn to overcome our difficulties and begin to live again. For those who never experience affirmation and belonging, this can be much more difficult.

If we live in a society that allows its members to be open, honest and caring, then we create a place where healing can take place and where the world of isolation is removed. But there are many people who feel excluded from this world of care. There are many who do not fit into our 'concept' of Church, family and community, and so we exclude them. Those who are different frighten us and fear breeds dissatisfaction, suspicion and eventual resentment. Fear finds all kinds of scapegoats, especially among people who are vulnerable. They can carry our guilt. We condemn people to lives of great pain and loneliness just because they are disabled, poor, mentally ill or gay, because we have a great fear within ourselves of who and what they are. We use gospel values to justify our own self-righteous prejudices. I remember feeding a young mother dying of AIDS in a slum in Africa and asking myself, 'Why, O why had I held such fear in my heart for so long?'

We build the walls of social stigma around us because we fear change or because we feel that to accept and love someone who is different will cause us problems. If we are not ready or prepared to give of ourselves, then we will find every reason to protect our *own* corner and our *own* possessions. We watch television and read media that show us the perfect way to live and look, and so we avoid what is ugly and disagreeable and we judge our standards by what people have achieved, rather than who they are at heart and what they *really* have to offer.

Of course, the antithesis of all of this is the way that Jesus treated human beings. He saw them as people with boundless potential against a horizon of goodness and equality, where everyone was unique but made in the image and likeness of His loving father. Jesus came to walk with us in our loneliness and to call us into communion with each other. He Himself knew loneliness, culminating in his great suffering on the night before He died – but that night was also the night in which He offered us a solution to loneliness. By washing the feet of His disciples, He offered a service of love and commitment for all to see, and by sharing the bread and wine, He invited us into communion with him, offering a place at the table to every one, even those who were about to deny Him and betray Him.

This call into communion with one another is the antidote of much of the self-centeredness that exists in the world today. It is the complete antithesis of the greed that has existed and that places the individual and his needs above the interests of the community.

It is, however, difficult to move into a relationship with others unless we have the capacity to be grateful. This is a gift that we must ask for, a grace that enables us to see the goodness of God in our lives and subsequently the goodness of God in the lives of those around us. Such goodness will include joy and sorrow, and weakness and failure, as well as achievement. These things are all the tools God uses to prune and prepare us for a future that can be inclusive of others, even those who are different, better, poorer or weaker than us. In his book *The Return of the Prodigal Son*, Henri Nouwen wrote:

> *The choice for gratitude rarely comes without some*
> *real effort. But each time I make it, the next choice is*
> *a little easier, a little freer, a little less self-conscious.*
> *Because every gift I acknowledge reveals another and*
> *another until finally, even the most normal, obvious,*
> *and seemingly mundane event or encounter proves*
> *to be filled with grace. There is an Estonian proverb*
> *that says, 'Who does not thank for little will not*
> *thank for much.' Acts of gratitude make one grateful*
> *because step by step, they reveal that all is grace.*

When I reflect on all the blessings I have received in my life, I can truly appreciate all that I have. I begin to realise that I *am* rich and that perhaps I have more than I ever thought possible. God has blessed me with so much, though I may not realise what I have been given and these things may not necessarily be valued in the eyes of the world. Jesus never worried about what people had or what position they held, rather, He cared about them, especially those who carried heavy life-sapping burdens. He brought His compassion into the places of darkness, to those who were consigned to the margins as outcasts, to the hideouts of lepers, to those bound by dark spirits, to those who were trapped by addictions, to those who were genuinely lonely and broken and especially to those who were rejected.

Jesus never left people in their places of pain. He called them into the light with new dignity and hope. The man who was born blind, the cripple lowered through the roof, the leper, the woman about to be stoned by her accusers and many more – all were called forth to be re-integrated into their communities and brought out of isolation and suffering. Jesus broke down prejudices and called people back into life *but* he also highlighted the prejudices of those who judged – the people who sent others into isolation. Jesus offered the transforming power of love to all.

When someone experiences acceptance and love, then little by little they have an opportunity to begin to heal and see life in a different way. It is not always easy but it can be life changing. The woman from Samaria who met Jesus at the well realised this and went home a very different person with her dignity restored. In those few moments of meeting, she was deeply moved by the sincerity of the one who had time for her and spoke to her, regardless of the taboos of the time and culture. She was very aware of her own shortcomings, but she was released from her difficult past to return home with a new outlook and new belief in herself! We don't know what happened to her after she returned home or about the direction her life took, but there are many instances of others who met Jesus, and how meeting Him was a transforming experience for them. It may have taken many years for the woman from Samaria to 'live' again, but she believed that she could and this is where the miracle takes place. Somewhere in the core of her being, she embraced the genuine love and care that Jesus had for her.

As Christians, this is the transforming, healing love that we are called to bring to others, so that they too can 'live' again. To do this means that we are called to accompany our brothers and sisters when they cannot walk the path of life alone any longer. For them, the road to freedom is the decision to reach out and cry for help; for us the road to coming closer to God is the decision to accompany another in their time of pain and suffering.

I have learned that each time I walk into locked psychiatric wards, my fear lessens as I began to see before me the gentle eyes of another human being. I have also learned that to be more Christ-like, I needed to trust more in God's presence, especially in my own deep places of fear and prejudice. As we are reminded in Romans 8: 'With God on our side who can be against us?' Such a trust, which can take a lifetime to really embrace, enables us to live lives of openness, without fear and worry. It is akin to what St Paul calls 'putting on the mind of Christ' so that we can see life through his lens.

Such trust also enables us to create a new vision for ourselves where our demons are consigned to the past and where we can begin to live with more compassion, more tenderness and gentleness, with more joy. We can begin to rediscover the beauty of the world that may have been seen for so long through grey eyes.

One summer evening, I went into the hospital to visit a young man who had been receiving treatment for depression. It was late in the afternoon and the sun was dancing high in the heavens and the gardens were teeming with colour and life. Through the hospital window, the warm rays danced across the room, casting warm shadows on the young man as he lay in bed. But he was so lost in his own pain that he could not experience the light of the day. He was in a place of deep depression, and I was exasperated within myself that I was unable to help his suffering. He loved music but because of his illness no song or tune was able to penetrate his place of inaccessibility. I sat with him and eventually left with a heaviness in my heart that someone so young and with his whole life ahead of him should be so burdened. The beauty of the day seemed to highlight the huge paradox of what was taking place.

I drove my car out to the foothills that surround the town I live in. As I drove, the colours of foliage and forest spread a bright green canvas all around, interrupted here and there by the yellow furze that was blooming all over like a hillside on fire. I parked my car and stood gazing down on the valley below. Beyond in regal solitude stood the mountains of Wicklow, majestic in a haze of blue and purple. The sun cast shadows on the valley floor and the only noise was the humming of flies and the intermittent song of a skylark who wandered overhead alarmed that I had interrupted his peace. I saw in the distance buildings, streets and a river. I saw the stories of these streets and the people who told them. I imagined the joys and sorrows continuing there below me and I saw the pain of the young man I had just left. I realised how blessed and fortunate I was not just to have what I had, but also to be in the privileged place of knowing such people and the good fortune to journey with them. I sat in my car and I listened to a piece of music from the American composer, John Michael Talbot. The music was melodic, beautifully orchestrated and powerfully contemplative. I thought and prayed for all the people I knew, who were imprisoned by depression, anxiety and guilt, and, in a moment of ultimate frustration, I wept.

But this was also a moment of epiphany for me. I realised that I could, and should, do much more to use what I had been given in the service of others. Up to that point, I had always told myself that I would like to write music, but I never did. When I was in college, I had written one piece of spiritual music but in the years that followed, I had written nothing. My insecurities had imprisoned me. As I sat in my car, I decided I had to try – I didn't know if I would be good, but at least I wouldn't go through life wondering if I should have made an effort, and regretting that I hadn't.

In the months that followed, I began to write and compose. When I was uncertain, as I was many, many times, I prayed for guidance and the hope that what I was expressing was not just my own self-serving journey but something that would help others from their places of pain and isolation.

On the night of my very first public performance, I saw an old man cry. I never found out who he was, but I realised the power of song, a divine gift, that can release us from that which haunts us and enable us to live again. That was twenty years ago, and the same experience has been re-lived over and over again as I witness God's amazing love, calling his children out of their prisons and into the light again.

I wrote my songs to touch the brokenness of others, but I am also touching the brokenness in my own life and needing the same Jesus to reach down and touch me in the gentle way He touched those who cried out to Him by the roadside. I do not always see Him but I am certain that, in time, He will reveal Himself in the broken wounds of another beautiful soul.

A Time to
Love, a Time
to Hate

He sat by the bed
Watching every movement
Of her tiny lips
Slowly listening to
The rhythm
Of each breath
Until his and hers became one
The child and the man ~

And somehow
He knew
That if God
Could create something
As beautiful as this little child
From the brokenness of His life
Surely He must love him.

ove and hate are probably the most challenging themes about which I have written, but in a book like this, they are impossible to avoid. It is very tempting to write about situations and examples on a universal scale, but that would be disingenuous. As human beings, we have all experienced the concepts of love and hate in our lives, and I am no different – I might like to think I am, but I am not!

Because we are human, we make mistakes. Our views differ, our cultures differ, our attitudes differ, our tastes differ – and so they should, otherwise our world would be a very boring place. These differences, combined with all the idiosyncrasies, injustices, desires and beliefs that we experience each day, can cause ruptures, pain and stress, even deep wounds that hurt us deeply. To counter such experiences and occurrences, we need to reconcile with ourselves and others, and we need 'forgiveness'. How we achieve this is another question, but even psychology has been able to prove its benefits, showing that if we want to move on with our lives to a healthier place, we need to embrace the concept of forgiveness.

I agree with this belief, but I also understand how people can find this journey extremely difficult and painful in practice, especially if they have been deeply hurt and wounded. We have many views about forgiveness and what it means. For Christians, we need only look at the life of Jesus to see the tremendous capacity He had to forgive throughout his life, culminating in His dying moments when, having been brutally treated and with excruciating effort, He cries out to God to forgive those who had done this to Him –'*Father forgive them, for they know not what they do*' – His words, so counter-cultural and misunderstood, have been rejected by many.

Forgiveness is a difficult concept for most people to grasp, because it can take a long journey to move towards it. I believe, from my own experience, that forgiveness is *not* about forgetting or about justifying or accepting an offence, nor is it about condoning or excusing a hurt or transgression or an injustice. For me, it is a wilful, conscious choice to turn away from the hurt, resentment and, anger that can draw us towards revenge and paralysis, arising from an experience of betrayal, injustice, pain and deep wound. It calls for a willingness to see the hurt or the injustice in a larger context, and to replace our negative feelings with compassion and tolerance, which are deeply rooted in our Christian belief.

In deciding to move from a place of paralysis and anger, we can also acknowledge that the offence was unfair, wrong and disrespectful, but that we are prepared to embrace a new possibility of change and restoration of our peace. This in no way mitigates my need for self-respect and fairness, to which we are always entitled. Forgiveness is an opportunity for transformation, both individually and collectively, as it offers the chance for change and a better future. So many times when we are experiencing a cycle of hurt and pain, we wish that it would stop. Forgiveness can help us achieve this. I believe that it offers an opportunity for healing and wholeness and can help us to experience a new capacity for compassion. In the words of Thich Nhat Hanh, the Buddhist teacher:

> *Forgiveness will not be possible until compassion is born in your heart.*

Sometimes, it can be easier to find examples of forgiveness that impress and affect us, especially if they are universal and well known. However, when it comes to taking the steps towards forgiveness in our own lives, we can find it much more difficult, especially if we have been deeply hurt, as so many have.

The journey to forgiveness is not an easy one and may take considerable time, but we take the first step

when we acknowledge that there is a need to forgive
or to reconcile. There is a saying in Chinese culture:

> *The giant pine tree grows from a tiny sprout. The*
> *journey of a thousand miles starts from beneath your*
> *feet.*

Forgiveness will always be more difficult for some
than for others. In my own ministry, I have met people
for whom the mere mention of the word 'forgiveness'
causes much anger; then there are others who are more
willing to begin to walk this road. Psychologists, who
have studied people's tendency to forgive, note that
there are personality traits that may predispose some
people to forgiveness, for example, how emphatic or
emotionally engaged we are with others. Obviously a
person's upbringing, genetic make-up, our community
values and our personality will all contribute to their
openness to forgive.

Forgiveness is a decision that in time can be
embraced, but we may need to begin at a lower level.
A good acid test is how we react to people in normal
circumstances – our ability and willingness to forgive
when, for example, our friends forget to do something
for us, or if someone lets us down or betrays our
confidence, or if someone annoys us while driving!
These are all fairly regular occurrences in people's
lives but how we react to them is a good indicator of
how we might incorporate forgiveness in our lives. If
we can make a conscious decision to deal with such

experiences in a more forgiving, compassionate way, then it enables us to develop a greater openness to those experiences, that really hurt us at a much deeper level.

As Christians, we are called to be people of forgiveness. Jesus challenges us to forgive our brothers and sisters not seven times but seventy times seven (Matthew 18:35). It sounds wonderful, but the actual practical application can be very different. This challenge is also reflected in the writings of Pope Benedict XVI:

> *We cannot communicate with the Lord if we do not communicate with one another. If we want to present ourselves to Him, we must also take a step towards meeting one another. To do this, we must learn the great lesson of forgiveness: we must not let the gnawing of resentment work in our soul, but must open our hearts to the magnanimity of listening to others, open our hearts to understanding them, eventually to accepting their apologies, to generously offering our own.*

So how do we begin this journey from a place of betrayal, hurt and anger to a place of acceptance and forgiveness? Thomas à Kempis, a fifteenth-century German Catholic monk, became well known for his spiritual writings. His book *The Imitation of Christ* became a masterpiece of his time and was widely read. He is attributed with the lines:

*First keep peace within yourself, then you can also
bring peace to others.*

This, I believe is the key to beginning this journey.
When I can begin to love and accept myself, then I can
begin to see others in a different light. Self-respect can
only lead to a healthier outlook in life and a greater
openness to reconciliation. This is one of the central
core values of Christian living. Even the Lord's prayer
underlines this:

*And forgive us our trespasses as we forgive those
who trespass against us.*

The book *Left to Tell* is the heartbreaking but amazing
story of Immaculée Ilibagiza, a Tutsi survivor of the
Rwandan genocide. Her father, mother and two
brothers were killed by the Hutus while she and seven
other women were able to escape and hide – crammed
into a tiny bathroom in the house of an Episcopalian
priest. For three months, they remained hidden,
hearing murderous Hutus gangs roaming in search of
Tutsis who had escaped the ethnic cleansing.

Day by day, hour-by-hour, she fought terror and
feelings of revenge by praying constantly. She prayed
the Rosary continually fighting the hatred with prayers
of healing and forgiveness. According to Immaculée:

*The people who'd hurt my family had hurt
themselves even more and they deserved my pity.*

There was no doubt that they had to be punished for their crimes against humanity and against God … but I prayed for compassion as well. I asked God for the forgiveness that would end the cycle of hatred – hatred that was always so dangerously close to the surface.

Eventually, she and the other women escaped but did so in very dangerous circumstances. She continued to pray for forgiveness for those who searched for her and who had destroyed her family and future. Eventually she came face to face with the man who had murdered her mother and brother, and who most likely would have killed her if he had found her, but she offered forgiveness:

I knew that my heart and mind would always be tempted to feel anger – to find blame and hate. But I resolved that when the negative feelings came upon me, I wouldn't wait for them to grow or fester. I would always turn immediately to the source of all true power: I would turn to God and let His love and forgiveness protect and save me.

Some people reading this may have great difficulty with Immaculée's forgiveness, asking why such horrific and barbaric cruelty should be met with forgiveness and compassion. Others may feel that the idea of forgiveness is in danger of becoming redcuced or trivialised in modern culture, that the call to forgive may demean the victim or downplay the crime. How can you forgive the unforgiveable? What role could forgiveness play in stopping horrors such as those that are happening in present-day Syria, for example, including state-sponsored terrorism and torture? How could forgiveness help people who have had their lives destroyed and affected terribly by systematic injustice from the highest levels?

Forgiveness requires us to cross many barriers – emotional, mental, ethical and even spiritual. It cannot be separated from the need for justice, emotional healing, grieving and mourning, and in some cases reconciliation and restitution. It can never trivialise the wrong that has been perpetrated, nor should it condone or absolve the evil that is visited on people's sacred lives. When people begin to cross this barrier, hope in the human condition can be restored, but there needs to be generosity of spirit on both sides and each story must be heard and respected.

So often, we can carry the burdens of hurt in our lives for long periods of time. The longer we hold on to this burden the less likely we are to forgive and the harder it becomes to face our demons. Similarly, if we ourselves need to be forgiven for something that we have done wrong, the more we procrastinate, the harder it will become to seek forgiveness. It takes courage to ask for help and forgiveness and it takes courage to accept the sorrow of another. Both demand humility and compassion. Sometimes, we are unable to make this journey alone. In my own life, I have been blessed with those who have journeyed with me, especially when I needed the support of objective voices and clear minds. Martin Luther King in his great struggle for human rights said:

> *We must develop and maintain the capacity to forgive. He who is devoid of the power to forgive is devoid of the power to love. There is some good in the worst of us and some evil in the best of us. When we discover this, we are less prone to hate our enemies.*

When I am in Ireland, I listen to the radio every day and I am more and more conscious of the need for healing and forgiveness within and for our country. So many people have had their lives completely destroyed and devastated by the endless nightmares of murder, addictions, abuse, financial debt, tragedy and brokenness at every level. So many people have been left wounded and hurting in an endless sea of despair while all the sacred cows – the institutions, whether they be those of the Church, State or banking systems, that people had put their trust in – have failed them. Sadly, popular culture often glorifies the notion of revenge. People want to seek revenge on behalf of those who have been hurt. But we need to move beyond this place of revenge and reprisal, otherwise it will paralyse our future and hand on a very dismal legacy to our children's children. Obviously we need to learn from the mistakes that have been made, and they need to be acknowledged, but seeking reconciliation and justice are separate choices and can be revisited at a later stage.

When I have spoken with people who have undergone great trauma or hurt in their lives, I always ask them to be gentle with themselves. It can be so difficult to begin to articulate our feelings and many tears may be shed before we can even begin to talk. Furthermore, it's not unusual for people to feel depressed or guilty when telling their story, but if we embrace the notion of forgiveness it can become one of our steps to healing as we try to move on from a deep hurt or experience in our lives. Every person is different and we all approach things in our own way.

One of the things that have helped me enormously in my own life has been my ability to express myself in my music, especially when life has been difficult and I have been let down or hurt by others. The outward expression of an inner tension offers a vehicle for healing that I have been very fortunate to know. Much of my music is spiritually based, so it becomes my prayer. Such an expression enables me to explore the themes of forgiveness, reconciliation and beauty which can be so lacking in a heart that is bent on revenge.

Some time ago, I was privileged to be invited to sing at a special Liturgy of Lament and Repentance for those who, as children, suffered sexual abuse by members of the clergy. It was a very painful and difficult experience, and even though I was profoundly moved and upset, I was glad to use my voice to pray and sing for healing. One of the prayers used was written by Brother Roger of Taize, a man of great peace who died so tragically himself:

Christ Jesus, Saviour of every life,
You take your burdens upon yourself
You suffer with all who bear the cross of suffering in
*   whatever form it takes*
So that, with you, we can move forward:
from worry and anxiety to trust, from darkness to
*   light.*

With you accompanying us, even what pains our
*   heart,*
Even our darkness can be made bright
By the inner light of the Holy Spirit.
You stretched out your arms on the cross
and reconciled us to one another and to the Father.
You brought God and humanity together in your
*   body.*
Wrap your arms around our broken lives
and restore us to the harmony that exists in you.

When the liturgy was over and people began to depart, I stood for a time in silence at the back of the cathedral, trying to absorb all that had happened but also believing that when we invite God into the brokenness of our lives, into the most vulnerable and sacred places, we open our lives to the possibility of healing, reconciliation and hope. The gospel stories are full of this – from the tears of Mary Magdalene to the repentant thief who is invited into paradise by Jesus because he has recognised his need for forgiveness.

Such forgiveness will bring a new freedom into our lives, and it begins with ourselves. Very often it's our lack of compassion for ourselves that makes us so upset with others and compassion is the gift of an open heart. And all things are possible with God.

If grass can grow through cement
Love can find you at every time in your life.

Cher

The compassion and ability to forgive of some can be an inspiration to us all. On a trip to view the prison on Robben Island, a friend and I found ourselves following in the footsteps of Nelson Mandela as we retraced his journey to this remote island off the coast of Cape Town, set in the wild Atlantic Ocean.

On the day we travelled, the sky was sea blue, cloudless and calm and reflected in the water as the boat glided gracefully along. Another day and another trip and another group of people. The crossing is a mere six miles and took less than an hour. The island appeared nearer and nearer and seemed quiet. It had been a leper colony and prison for centuries, but it wasn't until the 1960s that this island really came to national and international attention when it became the home of Nelson Mandela for eighteen of the twenty-seven years that he was imprisoned.

Alighting from the boat and in shackles, Mandela and his comrades would have been met by a group of warders and dogs who would have shouted at them, 'This is the island and it's here you will die.'

Locked in solitary confinement and only allowed out for thirty minutes exercise in the morning and the same in the afternoon, prisoners had no beds, just three blankets. Sometimes, they would be dragged out into the hallway freezing cold, to spend the night there. A prisoner could receive and write only one letter every six months. One visit was allowed and family members or those who were visiting had to write in advance for permission. For many families, the long trip was extremely costly and arduous. Some would travel for days to get to Cape Town and then travel by boat over to the island only to be told that the visit was cancelled and that they should reapply in another six months. They would have to turn around and leave, knowing their loved one was yards away locked up and denied any human contact. No doubt these prisoners longed just to see and hear their children, let alone embrace them.

We got off the boat and boarded a waiting bus. There was quiet music playing in the background but the only sound the prisoners would have heard was that of shackles as they faced their first day on Robben Island.

We walked through the high stone gates and were immediately met by a guide who was smiling. He told us that he himself had been a prisoner here. His story was no different than the stories of others who were incarcerated in this gulag. At times, I found myself staring at this man in disbelief as he began to relate his life story from the day he was sent to Robben Island, a place of intense heat and parching sun during the summers, but a place of bitter cold winds blowing in from a wild Atlantic in dark winter. It was an ideal place for banishment, a place to 'deep freeze' a prisoner so that the world would forget.

Each day, prisoners, who were only known by numbers, worked for hours breaking stones in a yard surrounded by a ten-foot high wall which hid the glorious view of the wild free ocean or the harbour of Cape Town in the distance, the place of freedom. If they were not breaking stones in the yard, the prisoners were marched to work in the lime quarries in conditions of extreme physical labour, with the result that many became blind through working for hours on end in the blinding sun. Our guide told us, 'Each day, we were forced to participate in humiliating rituals such as being stripped naked and violated. Very often death from starvation and disease occurred but deaths from being beaten were the most common.'

We walked indoors and it was hard to imagine the sheer brutality that took place in the now brightly painted building. The corridor led towards Nelson Mandela's cell. How many thousands of days did he walk here? Like myself, Mandela is a tall man, and so was unable to lie fully stretched, because the cell was too small. Staring through the bars on the window, he looked on to the bleak and black yard where he broke stone after stone, day after day, week after week, month after month, year after year and yet he says, 'There were many dark moments when my faith in humanity was sorely tested, but I could not and would not give myself up to despair – that's where lay defeat and death. Many nights' sleep were broken by the sound of menacing dogs who were brought into intimidate and search the cells.'

Our guide tells us, 'No prisoner was allowed to sing. No prisoner was allowed to whistle.' As I heard him speak, I could not but be reminded of the psalm from the Babylonian captivity, 'How we can sing the Lord's song in a strange Land?' But it was what he said next that touched me deeply.

'We are Africans and we love bread but because we were political prisoners, we were on the F Scale Diet, the most menial. For us, there was no bread, intentionally. How we longed for the sweet taste of bread, and the dream of eating it at home. But they denied us bread and yet they reminded us every day that they were Christian, that they prayed every day with their families, with their children when they went home to them – Give us this day our daily bread – but we were not part of the 'us', that would be given daily bread.'

I sat on the steps of the prison yard, trying to imagine the stark reality of a young teenager being arrested and thrown into this futureless place of despair.

'Nelson Mandela kept reminding us to keep our minds creative and especially to look after the younger boys who were imprisoned, less they become depressed or suicidal. We learned how to communicate by leaving messages in the toilets or in the bottom of the food trays and we knew the outside world was listening and watching. Ours was a struggle for dignity rather than survival.'

On the walls of the prison many prisoners have written their stories – stories of those lucky enough to survive and those not so lucky, who lost their lives in a place of great sadness. If these walls could talk, they would weep. Yet this is where courage was born, this is where apartheid met its end. This is where the dignity of the human soul overcame the pathetic and the evil. This is where the world would learn of reconciliation and hope. After twenty-seven years in captivity, Nelson Mandela was freed. On the 11 February 1990, he walked out of the gates a free man, his struggle for freedom over. In 1994, he became the President of South Africa, a far cry from the prisoner in the stone breakers' yard watched over by armed guards and menacing Alsatians.

Mandela's inaugural speech was pure poetry with words that spoke with dignity and sheer eloquence:

Our deepest fear is not that we are inadequate. Our deepest fear is that we are powerful beyond measure. It is our light, not our darkness that most frightens us. We ask ourselves, 'Who am I to be brilliant, gorgeous, talented, fabulous?' Actually, who are you not to be? You are a child of God. Your playing small does not serve the world. There is nothing enlightened about shrinking so that other people won't feel insecure around you. We are all meant to shine, as children do. We were born to make manifest the glory of God that is within us. It's not just in some of us; it's in everyone. And as we let our own light shine, we unconsciously give other people permission to do the same. As we are liberated from our own fear, our presence automatically liberates others.

I walked back to the bus and waited for our guide who was coming to say goodbye. I wanted to ask him so much and yet I wanted to be respectful. But there was one question that was burning inside of me that I did need to ask him. We walked and, kicking the pebbles in the way, I turned to him and asked, 'Why did you forgive? And how can you come and walk and work here among those who stole your dignity. How can you look at them face to face and not want revenge?'

It seemed that he was waiting for this question all these years or perhaps he has heard it so often. In my asking came all the hurts, all the pain of my own life and all the injustices that I had known, and may have even caused others.

'I can forgive because if I don't it becomes my cancer, my problem, my hurt and you see, Sir, I have had enough hurt in my life. So I made a decision that I would not resort to hate, to bitterness, to revenge, and now, now I am free, I am happy. I can see the world in a different way.' He shook my hand, smiled and was gone.

The waters lapped the side of the boat and the afternoon breeze lifted but the air was not so heavy. I tasted the sweet taste of freedom and on the wind I heard the voice of a free man:

> *Never, never and never again shall it be that this*
> *beautiful land will again experience the oppression*
> *of one by another.*
> Nelson Mandela

A Time
for Peace

There is no tongue
That cannot speak of peace
There is no hand
That cannot offer Peace
There is no heart
That cannot harbour peace
There is no mind
That cannot long for peace ~

For you, the Prince of peace
Walked among us
Calling us from places of
Revenge
Hate
Into the shelter of your forgiving Peace

May all who would lift
An arm against another
Be confronted by the
Compassion of Your eyes
That knows the pained desire
Of all of life's wounded
And your open hands
Offering the loving kindness
Of the heart of our
God.

song of mine that I am frequently asked about is 'How Can I Heal Your Broken Heart?', which I wrote in response to the cataclysmic tsunami which struck the coast of Asia and claimed hundreds of thousands of lives on the 26th December 2004. It was like an Asian Armageddon, as cities and islands were swept away by the deadly waters. In the days that followed, I was asked to join an artist and a writer for a programme of remembrance to be broadcast on national radio, which would express the grief of our nation through the various media in which we worked.

I reflected much on what had happened and decided that I would like to write a piece to express my deep sorrow and sympathy for all those affected. I was still trying to find adequate words when something caught my eye whilst I was watching Sky News. The reporter was relaying a story from Indonesia when a very distressed man came up to him and began to pull on his arm, trying to take him somewhere. The camera followed them to a wall, which was covered in photographs of missing people. The man, who was clinging to the reporter, began to wail and weep as he pointed to a photograph of a young boy of about ten who has been missing since the wave hit the island. What followed was extremely poignant, as the man, forgetting about the camera and the reporter, began to speak directly to the little boy's photo, pleading, 'Why don't you come home? Your mother and I are so worried. Where are you? Please come home.'

As I watched this tragic story, coming live into my living room, I wished that the reverse could happen – that I could have reached out to this man and offered consolation and sympathy, and held him as he wept for his young son. Sitting at my piano, I wrote:

> *How can I heal your broken heart*
> *When all of the pieces are fractured apart?*
> *And though it may seem that we're worlds afar*
> *I pray you'll find someone*
> *I pray you'll find someone*
> *Who will hold you through the dark.*

From there, the report moved to another image that was beautifully symbolic. In a park with a lake, thousands of people had gathered, all wearing white, the symbol of mourning. They were lighting tiny night lights and candles and floating them on the lake, offering light to the souls of the departed on their way to Heaven. It was a beautiful and consoling scene that inspired the words:

Into the sky may your soul float on high
May the Angels be your guides.

When I sing this song, I re-imagine the scenes of those days and the utter devastation that occurred in people's lives and homes, but I also am aware of the huge outpouring of goodness and kindness that people showed in the aftermath of the tsunami.

I have no doubt that when we pray for others and wish peace for them, God hears our prayers and answers accordingly. When I am conscious of the world around me, of the brokenness and the need for healing, I am not detached but am fully alive to what is happening. My prayer can help the transformation of the world if I have a spirit of peace. In my prayer, I become conscious of all humanity – of my brothers and sisters, wounded, grieving, suffering, being born or dying – and I am in unity with everyone. I ask Jesus, the prince of peace, to be present to all. Being mindful of the present moment helps me to attend to the now, and to be focused on what is happening now. I entrust these moments to God, and pray for his peace. Thomas à Kempis, the great mystic of the Church, taught us:

First keep peace within yourself, then you can also
bring peace to others.

When I bring such situations into the silence of my prayer in sincerity, God always listens to my pleas and petitions. This is the great paradox – that when I go into the silence of my heart, into the place where God dwells, and am alone, I actually draw closer to others, to all of humanity, to my brothers and sisters. It leads me to a greater unity and harmony with the world, because it enables me to be in touch with my own humanity, my own fragility. And God is present, teaching compassion, concern and empathy. The peace that He offers becomes a peace for all the world, and in this silence, as my candle burns brightly, it not only casts light into my corner, but the light contributes to the light of the world, in its time of darkness.

When compassion becomes who we are, its effects are boundless, as it opens our eyes to the realities that much of the world cannot see, or simply chooses not to. I truly believe that peace is possible through compassion. When we rise above the narrow confines of our own needs and begin to look outwards, we are on the first step to creating a better world. Compassion becomes a way of life that can bring peace to all the situations of stress and turmoil that we meet. Our brother or sister in need or in trouble is not a nuisance or responsibility, but rather an opportunity to encounter the sufferings and needs of others. I may also be weak and fragile, but my willingness to touch the wounds of others is nothing more than what Christ would do.

What we think we are giving to others will always come back to us a thousandfold! I have experienced this so many times, and it has been the inspiration of much of my music – when I touch the wounds of others, I am always enriched in my own poverty.

Some time ago, I was invited to a weekend music conference being held at Minsteracres, an eighteenth-century mansion house in Northumberland, England, which is now a retreat centre run by the Passionist Order. Driving up the long avenue gives a wonderful sense of what life might be like there 300 years ago, when the original home was built. Set in the rural countryside, I looked forward to sharing music and prayer in this idyllic setting with a group of 130 people whom I had never met before.

After supper on the Friday evening, I gave a recital and introduced my work in the beautiful ballroom of the original house. I sat by the grand piano surrounded by gilt-edged mirrors in a long spacious room, and I imagined elegant ladies with their ball gowns swishing the floor under the shadows of a thousand candles as they danced to cheerful English folks songs under the watchful eye of an older generation.

As I began to perform, the end door of the ballroom opened and a young woman walked in quietly. As the ballroom was quite big, most of the audience were seated at the far end. I kept singing but, from the corner of my eye watched this woman standing and staring in my direction before she quietly walked out. For some reason, I was very conscious of her presence, even though she was not part of our group. The following day after a full morning, I took some time to visit the ancient monastic site of Lindisfarne, or Holy Island as it is also known, which is not far from Minsteracres. Reached at low-tide, it is a seventh-century monastic site founded by St Aidan, an Irish monk who had come from Iona off the west coast of Scotland. Around 700 AD, a beautiful illustrated book for the gospels, called the Lindisfarne Gospels, was written and the original copy can be seen today in the British Library in London.

Visiting Lindisfarne was an opportunity to explore the richness of the tradition within our Church about which so many people today are unaware. The beauty of these gospels gives a rare insight into the spirituality and the craftsmanship of these early monks, and also of their close relationship with their natural surroundings. They were never far from danger, as is seen from the history and accounts of the violent ransacking of the monasteries by the Vikings in the eighth century. How the Lindisfarne Gospels and many other precious artefacts of this era survived is a credit to the monks themselves and their great efforts to protect these priceless treasures.

The woman who had walked in and out of my performance the previous night, was one of the few people who travelled with me to walk the sands of Lindisfarne, but I still knew nothing of her story. After another workshop in the afternoon, the group came together in the evening to share songs and stories and to relax. I always enjoy listening to music that is indigenous to a particular area.

The following morning after some final preparation,

we celebrated the Eucharist before our departure. It was a beautiful liturgy and very edifying to hear the people sing the music we had been rehearsing all weekend with such zeal and prayerfulness. At one stage, my eye caught some of the people present and, there among them, was the same young woman whom I had seen on the very first night. As we prayed, I looked down and saw that she was weeping.

When the Eucharist was over, I went into the sacristy to remove my vestments as I had been the celebrant.I heard a knock on the door and, as I opened it, standing there was this same woman. I invited her in. She appeared to be drying her eyes, then, very politely and softly, she began to speak.

Her name was Lya Vollering and she was from a small village near Utrecht, in Holland. Having studied politics, she had been accepted to work as an international observer in Guatemala, a country that has suffered a very difficult recent history in which over 20,000 indigenous people have lost their lives. Many of those who died were Mayan Indians, who lived in the mountains and rural areas and had suffered great injustices being caught up in the struggle for freedom.

In 1999, a Guatemalan truth commission blamed the army for 93 per cent of the atrocities and the rebels (the Guatemalan National Revolutionary Unit) for 3 per cent. The former guerrillas apologised for their crimes, and President Clinton apologised for the US's support of the right-wing military governments. The army has not acknowledged its guilt. Alfonso Portillo

Cabrera became president in January 2000 and, eight months later, in August, he apologised for the former government's human rights abuses and pledged to prosecute those responsible and to compensate victims. It was against this background that Lya began to work as an international observer.

After working with the UN for seven months, she decided to work for a truth commission set up by the Catholic Church, which aimed to enable some healing and closure for the people who had seen and suffered so much. Lya told me:

> *If you want peace, you need to give people an opportunity to tell their story, to tell what had happened. So many people were forced to kill their neighbours, friends – all done when mistrust and untruths were spread so wrongly. The truth commission sought to try and help people to restore trust and confidence.*

Even though I was in the middle of the beautiful Northumbrian countryside, I was engaged by the intensity of Lya's story and was immediately immersed in the foothills of Guatemala. Lya continued, 'One of the words that I learned immediately, as I had heard it so much was the word 'k'aix'. This is the Mayan word for pain, especially emotional suffering. It seemed to be heard in almost every conversation.'

The work that Lya undertook was to help to plan and co-ordinate the search for those who had disappeared as well as the subsequent exhumation of the bodies. She continued her story:

One day, a woman came to us to ask us to search and exhume her son and her husband. They, like many of the victims, had died by being gunned down or brutally cut down with machetes, as could be seen from the wounds inflicted on the remains. She could not rest until she had found them and given them a proper burial. Dreams are very important in the Mayan tradition, especially among the women, and this woman believed that her son and husband could not rest until they were given a proper Christian burial. So began the search for this woman's husband and son.

Lya's eyes told of her pain as she reconnected with those days.

You know, I thought of the words of Etty Hillesum, a young Jewish woman whose letters and diaries, kept between 1941 and 1943, describe life in Amsterdam during the German occupation and who died in Auschwitz, in Poland. In one of her diaries she wrote:

There's a really deep well inside me. And in it dwells God. Sometimes I am there too. But more often stones and grit block the well, and God is buried beneath. Then (God) must be dug out again.

The image of digging God out from beneath the rubble was so real for me as I grappled with the terrible reality of searching for the bodies of young children and their fathers in the clay beneath us. The inhumanity of man becomes so striking when you are faced with such a terrible reality.

As I tried to begin work, we were asked to go to a place called Las Joyas (the Jewel). These were caves set at the edge of the village that had been used during a horrific slaughter of young children, boys and men. The people had come out of the mountain villages to meet the military, thinking that the soldiers were coming to help them but, instead, the villagers were rounded up and brought to Las Joyas and never seen again.

One of the mothers came to us, her name was Maria and she was searching for her son Diego who had been executed by the death squads at Los Joyas. It had been fifteen years since the deaths at Los Joyas had taken place and, when exhumed, the bodies were simply bones, though they still had some of the clothes. Many were identified, but some were not. Maria spoke of a significant dream of her son, who had come here wearing particular clothes. He seemed very happy and told her not to worry about him. She later recognised his body by the same clothes she had seen in her dream.

We found a number of bodies in Las Joyas. I remember the caves were very dark and I was haunted by the terrible grief and suffering within this dark confined space. On one side were the families of the deceased, absolutely desperate to find their own loved ones; on the other, the mounds of earth that piled up in the search. There was no natural light only candlelight. Can you imagine the distress of opening a grave?

She opened a book that she had brought with her and showed me some photographs taken as a record of what was taking place. In the photographs, I saw a mother being held back from a grave, her arms held out in unbearable grief, trying to reach down to touch the body of her young son. When he had been exhumed, there was a toy in his little hand. Lya tells me that difficult as this work was, 'You had to open the graves to bring some rest and healing to these poor people. People sharing each other's pain. At least some of them found the bodies of their loved ones, but, sadly, others did not. In one grave, we found the body of an eighty-year-old man. He was still wearing a colorful handkerchief just as my own father did. It was so humbling to share such grief with these people.'

After the search, twenty-nine bodies were found at Las Joyas, after which the ritual of preparing them for reburial was started. Among the Mayan people, such rituals are very respectful – the bodies were redressed in new, clean and colourful clothes. They were all lined up in the church alongside each other. Each grave held an identified body and an unidentified one, so that families could look after both of them. On each coffin was written:

'Nuestro Hermano – Our Brother.'

Lya then described how she continued to work in this role for another three years, to help bring some closure to the families who had suffered so much.

It was indeed a very special privilege to share in such intimate suffering with these people, but it took its toll. Every day, I would see more and more suffering and enter the realm of anticipation as families dug desperately to find their children, their husbands, brothers or fathers. And when they did, what an outpouring of grief and loss. We cried for lost years, for lost lives, for lost love. What cruelty of man to man – to murder young children or their fellow countrymen! At night, I would be so haunted by what I experienced during the day. I tried to sleep but, so often, the faces of the people would frequent my dreams. One day, I took a break went to stay with a friend of mine who was also from Holland. She and her husband were also working in Guatamala on a different project. They knew how difficult my work was for me and how I was struggling with the impact of the work I was doing. One night, her husband handed me a cassette tape and told me that it might help me to sleep. I fell asleep listening to the voice and the words that seemed to resonate with what was happening for me. It brought me comfort and ease.

After a few days rest with my friends, I returned

to the mountains to continue my work with the truth commission and to continue the exhumations. As I was leaving, my friend gave me the casette to take with me and every night, haunted by the day, I would fall asleep listening to the voice and the music.

After three years of this work, I knew it was time to leave. Such experiences take their toll and tell their own story. It was very difficult to leave the people I had come to know and love, but I knew that for my own sake I had to take some time to rest and recuperate after the challenges of such work. So I came home to Holland but I found it difficult to settle down. I was coming from a very different world, so difficult to describe to anyone but you carry always much in your heart. A friend of mine suggested that I come to visit the Passionist Monastery here at Minsteracres, so I did, to get some rest and to try and de-stress and reflect on all that had happened.

I arrived on Thursday evening and, on Friday, I went for a walk after supper. When I came back into the building, I thought I could hear some music, I knew there was a conference beginning. I was sitting in the lounge when, suddenly, I heard a voice singing. I said to myself: That's strange, but I feel as if I know this voice, but I did not know how. So I listened again and eventually I followed the sound of the voice and I walked into the ballroom. As I stood there, I realised that the voice I was listening to was the same voice that I listened to every night in Guatemala. It was like a circle was closing, but I could only stay for a few moments and I had to leave because so many memories began to flood back to me – they were so strong!

I saw before me again the mothers, the children, the suffering, the broken hearts – so much pain and yet so much beauty and compassion. I needed to be alone to take it all in. Listening to your voice was like being followed from Guatemala, and I realised that I too needed healing and closure, just like the broken people that I had met over there. The wounds of others will always be reflected in our brokenness.

Since I heard your voice on Friday night, I have been thinking of the many faces and situations that I have seen. Today, when we celebrated the Mass, I brought them all to the Lord and I prayed for peace – for all of them and for myself too, that my memories too would find rest and peace.

I stood in the sacristy, deeply moved by Lya's story. Nine years later, I remember every detail and I can still see the images that she showed me. I asked her how she came across my music, and she explained how her Dutch friend had married an Irishman, who had carried the music with him to Guatemala. We speak of one of the songs that she listened to – 'The Darkest Hour', which I had written about the suffering people of Ireland during the famine. How apt its words seemed to Lya:

The darkest hour when land no more would flower
The darkest hour when life's sweet taste was sour
Who knows the hour – the darkest hour.

And will there be remembering for those who died
*   in vain*
And will there be a song to sing to soothe the cry of
*   pain*
To green the earth again.

And will there be remembering of skies that knew
*   no sun*
Of winds that blew through leafless trees, of birds
*   that never sung*
O poor forgotten one.

And shall we sleep remembering the night that knew
*   no end*
When life's sweet hope was vanishing because we
*   knew no friend*
T'was death we did befriend.

The darkest hour when land no more would flower
The darkest hour when life's sweet taste was sour
Who knows the hour – the darkest hour.

It had been nine years since I spoke to Lya and I have
often wondered what happened to her. I know that she
had stayed for a while in Minsteracres as a counsellor,
but then I lost contact with her. When I was writing

this book, I decided that I would very much like to include her story, so I called Minsteracres hoping to find out where I might contact her. I was so delighted to discover that she was still working there and very involved in a number of things, including a new project working with refugees who have been affected by torture. I am so humbled by her concern and compassion for other human beings and for her ability to spend her life caring for complete strangers in one hand and, in the other, accepting them as her brothers and sisters. 'How we live our lives is so important, every aspect. We all have our roles to play, everyone.' As we speak, Lya then tells me that she returned to Guatemala two years ago.

> *I needed to go there again. This time, it was very different but for myself I had to visit some of the significant places. And yes we went to the caves at Las Joyas. This time I took, a friend who is a priest, with me and we celebrated a prayer service at the mouth of the cave as an act of thanksgiving. It was beautiful and the air was light and free. And in respecting the Mayan beliefs and culture, we asked permission of God, of the dead and of Mother Earth, to take these precious souls to Himself so that they could rest forever in the loving arms of God.*

In the dream of God, there are many journeys, and each of us has our own path to follow. Sometimes, our paths will cross with others, in ways we least expect.

At these times, God will reveal a little more of His beauty, His compassion and His love for humankind and if we are fortunate and humble enough, we might recognise Him. Then we can offer the same to others, and once again peace will be born anew. People like Lya Vollering offer such peace and compassion in a broken world, sometimes when all hope is lost and through such empathy, fractured hearts can begin to dream again of a new tomorrow.

A TIME
TO EMBRACE

On winter nights
When snow-old winds blow bitter
Across a frozen sky
And memories huddle
In the corner of an ageing mind
May we remember
The tiny cry of a Bethlehem child
Heard by lonely shepherds
And heard in every heart
That longs to know the mystery of love ~
For God so loved that world
That he sent his only Son among us.

December was hardly born when an age-old ritual that welcomed in the season of Advent took place before dawn on a frosty winter's night. I had just become a seminarian and knew nothing of this old tradition when the choir rose before the dawn and gathered in the centre of St Joseph's Square in the beautiful old campus of Maynooth College. In my deep sleep, I suddenly heard the plaintiff tones of an ancient Latin text sung in four part harmony:

> Jerusalem, Jerusalem convertere ad Dominum Deum tuum.
> (Jerusalem, Jerusalem turn back to the Lord your God.)

For a few moments, I wondered if I was experiencing the beatific vision and had entered the realms of

Heaven, but then I heard laughing and shouting as the rest of the student body remembered that this was the night for the choir to sing the Advent motet. For newcomers like myself, it was a beautiful experience as each note echoed and re-echoed throughout the halls and buildings, reminding the world that soon an amazing event would take place and that we should prepare our hearts and lives. Every first night of Advent since, I have revisited that place in my heart, and every star-lit sky that shines down lights the way of memory and simple truth of Bethlehem's beauty.

For me, December is a busy month for travelling, performing and coming home to the community in which I live to celebrate the feast of Christmas. It is also a time, for all of us, to catch up with family and friends and to reconnect with the important people in our lives. Performing in so many communities throughout the country at this time gives me an opportunity to see the best of kindness and graciousness of the Irish spirit, but also the challenge to keep the real meaning of Christmas alive in a society that is ever more secular and cynical of the real Bethlehem story.

And yet there is something within the Irish spirit that recognises the importance of this season and its connection with a truth beyond our understanding. Why is it that most people will come to church at Christmas more than any other time of the year? Is it saying something about the deep longing that is within us humans, to connect with something greater than us, as we try to cope with the difficulties of life, the injustices all around us, the emptiness and loneliness that invades every community?

In a world of great technological advances and power-hungry personalities, what could we possibly find attractive in the Christmas story? For centuries, the people of Israel waited for their Messiah. Would He come in a blaze of glory and remove all that stood in His way? Would He cause fear and trembling and show the might of Heaven to the heathen? Would His personality be so charismatic that even the most cynical would be drawn to Him?

The imagination of God is far greater than this. Instead, He allowed Himself to become one of us in the most fragile, weakest of all – a tiny child, lying in a manger in a stable. He couldn't speak, he couldn't walk, he couldn't do anything except sleep and cry and hold on, with complete trust, to his loving mother. And only a few poor shepherds understood! They recognised him with the help of angels while the rest of the world laughed with scepticism. 'Surely God would never come this way?' God came among us almost unnoticed.

And yet, He did come. He came in innocence, in simplicity, in a non-threatening, vulnerable way, that overpowered all who came into contact with Him. Some even wanted to kill him, so great was His effect on them.

This is the true meaning of Christmas, meeting the vulnerable, the simplicity and the beauty of God manifest in a tiny, helpless child – not in the way we might have imagined. Saviours are supposed to be much stronger, much more powerful, much more assertive, but, for us, God is still depending on our help, our protection, our willingness to find a place for him, still waiting for the invitation.

In ancient Ireland, the people knew that gift of hospitality and desire to find a place for God made man. One of the beautiful traditions at Christmas is to light a candle in the window so that the Holy Family on their way to Bethlehem just might pass their way. The light in the window is a sign of welcome, a sign to the world that Christ was welcome in *this* home.

When I was a young boy, we would gather in our home on Christmas Eve and light the Christmas candle for the window. It was always lit by the youngest member of the household and we ended our prayer by saying: '*Go mbeirimid beo ar an am seo aris*' (*may we be all well and healthy this time next year*). Then the lighting candle would be placed in the window and right throughout the neighbourhood, the flickering candles of different homes brought a warm glow on a cold frosty night, and a welcome guidance on our way to Midnight Mass.

There are many voices heard at this time of the year. When I think of Christmas, I remember the sound of Christmas carols being sung. Every year our school choir went carol singing in the weeks before Christmas. Each night, we would go to a different area in the neighbourhood and sing at the end of the street. People would go from door to door collecting for the

Society of St Vincent de Paul and neighbours would gather to hear us sing all the beautiful old and new carols. But there was something else about this that was important. In the days before Christmas, it called people to stop and listen, to be aware and attentive to what was soon to happen. Perhaps in the craziness of secularism, we have lost the sense of this *time out*, given that we are so busy being busy. The singing of the carols was an opportunity to pause and in the silence of a December night allow a word or a line of an ancient carol to penetrate our hearts:

> *What can I give him poor as I am?*
> *If I were a shepherd I would bring a lamb*
> *If I were a wise man I would do my part*
> *Yet what I can I give him, give my heart.*

Christmas unmasks the real questions within our lives, and, for some, it can become a time of unrest and disturbance. Why are so many people lonely at this time of year while at the same time sing 'All is calm, all is bright'? Many people would rather wake up the day after Christmas Day than live through the experience of being alone, or without loved ones, for those twenty-four hours. There is something paradoxical about how the celebration of the birth of a child can cause so much isolation and pain. And yet this tiny child comes, not to bring pain and restlessness, but to bring hope and joy. He is the son of God, the gift of the Spirit, the created of the creator, the child of peace.

Christmas confronts us with the challenge – we either resign ourselves to tinsel and superficiality, mixed with mistletoe and wine, or we try and grasp the real meaning of Christ's coming among us into the turmoil that is humankind, to challenge us, revolutionise our thinking, our way of looking at the world and our faith, and change our way of treating our brothers and sisters.

Christmas is about the birth of hope. Despite the bleakness of the night, a child *was* born as one of us, and *eventually* His cry was heard. At first, it was only shepherds who recognised Him but then gradually the greater world came to hear of the Bethlehem story. The Magi, or wise men, came also in search of this child but on finding him, they 'went home a different way' – to a different life that would never be the same again.

Others became jealous and were threatened by this tiny baby and wanted to be rid of him because they could not humble themselves before Him; then, there were others still who were completely apathetic and didn't even try to embrace the mystery that was unfolding before them. In the space of 2,000 years, things have not changed an awful lot and, in the western world especially, the story of Bethlehem is becoming more and more obscured. People complain about the way Christian symbolism has been replaced with secular language and symbols, but perhaps as Christians our challenge is not to waste time and energy on such things, but rediscovering for ourselves the immensity and the great gift of wonder and awe, so that we too might truly recognise Christ when He comes among us.

How do we do this?

I believe that we need to reclaim the meaning and significance of Advent.

Advent comes from the Latin word *'adventus'* meaning 'coming', and is the time of preparation for the celebration of the birth of Jesus. It continues through the four Sundays before Christmas and it also signifies the second coming of Christ, so it is a time of waiting and hope. In ancient times, many cultures used this time to prepare for Christmas spiritually, and Ireland was no different.

In the farming community, the sheds and outhouses, walls and gates were all whitewashed and new bedding was put down for the animals. This period of fasting, penance and labour preparation was reflected also in the life of the Church, where the prayers and scriptural readings waited in longing for the coming of Emmanuel, God with us.

By the time Christmas Day came, the wonder of the season and the birth of the long awaited saviour was truly celebrated.

Through frost-tinted windows, the Bethlehem star could shine and the holy family of Nazareth could make their way down any boreen or country road on their way to find the stable. Such was the beauty and breadth of imagination that enabled such mystery to dwell in the hearts and minds of a people who knew

the importance of waiting and who were humble
enough to believe that perhaps God's heavenly plan
included them.

In contemporary times, our desire for immediate
satisfaction has consigned the season of Advent
somewhat to the past, and the expectant joy of the
season is buried under a deluge of crass materialism
and hollow jingles where the post-Christmas sales
become more important than any serious reflection of
the real meaning of Christmas. Yet the more we have,
the more we want – and the emptier our lives seem.
It is for this very reason that God becomes one of us,
and with his birth comes the birth of possibility – the
possibility of change, the possibility of hope. We can
sleep through each Christmas and allow it to be for
children only, or we too can embrace an opportunity
to contemplate the transcendent and take the risk to
allow Heaven to illuminate our world and our hearts.

Meister Eckhart, the medieval mystic, wrote:

> *What good is it to me*
> *If this eternal birth of the Divine Son*
> *Takes place unceasingly*
> *But does not take place within myself?*

> *And*
> *What good is it to me*
> *For the Creator to give birth to his/ her son*
> *If I do not wish to give birth to him*
> *In my time and in my culture?*

This then is the fullness of time
When the Son of God
Is begotten in us.

Being on tour for most of December, I have been privileged to partake in the preparations for Christmas within many communities over the years and to support many charities. Last December, we had a concert in Dublin to help the Christmas Day Dinner for homeless people, and I was overwhelmed by the support and the kindness of people particularly around this charity. There is a deep innate sense of compassion within the Irish psyche and this fact has been borne out many, many times in recent years when it comes to reacting to catastrophe and disasters at home and abroad. Peering in through the windows of various committees and supporting the various charities has given me a good insight into Irish life and values. True, in the years of Celtic Tiger madness, there were signs of crass superficiality and greed but amongst ordinary decent people, there has always been a deep sense of responsibility and concern, especially when people are suffering, as we have seen in so many incidences, in so many communities over the years.

At the end of my touring, I always return to the parish of St Clare's in Graigcullen. This is where I celebrate Christmas with the faith community who gather there. There are two traditions that I have adhered to and which mean much to me on Christmas Eve. The local parish community gathers for the Christmas Eve Vigil

Mass. The beautiful church is bedecked with holly wreaths and deep red poinsettias interspersed with candles and night-lights, transporting those who come into an oasis of peace and tranquillity.

Before the Mass begins, the local choir gather to sing age-old Christmas carols by the tall Christmas tree, which is always near the altar. The children have already had their special Christmas Mass and are tucked up in bed waiting excitedly for Santa Claus. My colleague Fr John usually celebrates and I will concelebrate with him while my other colleague, Fr PJ, celebrates in an outlying parish. The people, our neighbours and friends, gather to acknowledge and celebrate the birth of Jesus among us in our community.

For some, it will be a time of great joy, family reunion and excitement lived through the eyes of their children; for others, a time of sadness and loneliness as perhaps this is the first Christmas without a loved one. This time can be a stark reminder of the love we miss and cherished. For some, it will be a time of great stress and strain as unemployment and financial worry is heightened, as families and parents want to give the best to their children and are unable to do so.

But coming together as a faith community into the house of God, we are all equal, all one in the eyes of God – rich, poor, young, old, abled, disabled, national, non-national, straight, gay, employed or unemployed, man or woman – the helpless child born in a stable makes no distinction but reaches His tiny hands out, in intimacy for all. There is no judgement in His eyes and no fear in His heart. In this child is born compassion, peace and the willingness to mend broken lives. When the child was born, some came to the manger and knelt down, others walked away unable to accept the God-made-man, and others still offered all they had and went home a different way, seeking to change the world having changed themselves. It takes humility to walk up and kneel before the manger.

In the weeks before Christmas, on Advent days, I have sung in many churches with many choirs but there is always something special about singing with your own faith community, though at times I feel more self–conscious! And so with the lights dimmed, by candlelight and our focus on the manger, I sing the beautiful, well-loved carol 'O Holy Night'. This beautiful French carol embodies the rich meaning of this night in its soaring melody and heart-felt plea:

Fall on your knees O hear the angels voices
O night Divine O Night when Christ was born
O Night Divine O Night when Christ was born

When our Mass is ended, the families return home and continue their preparations for the following day. The scent of incense still hovers as, outside in the night air, the shining stars reflect on the diamond frost that shimmers on the windowpanes. I leave the church and cross the yard to enter the monastery of the contemplative Poor Clare Sisters whose foundation has been in the parish for almost 200 years. Every

Christmas Eve, I celebrate Midnight Mass within the heart of this haven of peace. This is far from the madness of bustling shoppers and endless queues. Christmas lights are replaced by red Christmas candles nestling in freshly cut holly, lighting the windows of the cloister, throwing flickering shadows on the whitewashed walls.

The sisters gather in the cloister where we walk before we enter the chapel. I am reminded of some lines from the contemplative Thomas Merton's 'After the Night Office':

> *We do not see the brothers bearing lanterns*
> *Sink in the quiet mist, as various as the spirits*
> *Who, with lamps, are sent to search Our souls'*
> *Jerusalem ...*

In the cloister, I carry the child Jesus in my arms, wrapped in white, ahead of the sisters as they process, carrying candles and singing 'The Wexford Carol', one of the ancient Irish Christmas carols, pausing at the corners of the cloister, pondering the silent mystery of this night::

> *Good people all this Christmas time*
> *Consider well and bear in mind*
> *What our good God for us has done*
> *In sending his beloved son*
> *With Mary holy we should pray*
> *To God with love this Christmas day*

In Bethlehem that very morn
There was a blessed Messiah born.

The origins of this carol are found in the twelfth century in the Wexford region and its striking imagery, coupled with the weight of tradition, finds a comfortable home within these hallowed walls. The voices echo and re-echo throughout the building, linking with the prayers and voices of souls from generations past who marked this holy night. Passing through the corridor, we enter the chapel. I remember the first time I entered this chapel on my first Christmas. Then (as now) I was overwhelmed with the simple beauty of the place and the beautiful Bethlehem scene, hand-painted by Sr John Francis who has since gone to her eternal reward. Placing the child in the manger, I place all the cares, worries and prayers of all who I carry in my heart. There is something warm and welcoming in the fresh winter straw as Mary and Joseph gaze lovingly on the Christ child. In the distance, a light casts shadows on a painted scene of Bethlehem and the inns and houses where there was no room. Here in this manger, the child is placed between the ox and ass, as he has done for almost 200 years. This winter night is no different.

The Mass is celebrated in quiet simplicity by candlelight. There is time and room to reflect on the mystery of the incarnation. We take our places before the manger and we pray for the community, the parish, our families and our world. I think of all the souls who have blessed my life knowingly and unknowingly in the past year. I think of all of the families who have been bereaved since we sang our carols a year ago. I think of all the miles travelled, all the songs sung, *all* the people of inspiration who have truly blessed my life. I think of all who travel with me. I remember all who are hurting, angry, alone, despairing. I think of my family – my brothers and sister, and their families – and I think of my own mother and father, who gave life to us and watched over our cradle. The mystery of the incarnation is for *all* time, for *all* people. It makes the impossible possible, the unworthy worthy and it tell us that Christ came for all people, no matter who or where.

It seems right and correct to sing 'Silent Night' within this place. Here the silence is merely a continuation of the eternal silence that existed before the world ever was, in the dream of God. But such silence is at the heart of our Church and is so necessary for our world. It is this silence that calls the contemplatives to spend Christmas day 'with the Lord', as the rest of the world celebrates and feasts. Their day is spent in silent adoration like the shepherds and the Magi at the Bethlehem stable.

As the Midnight Mass ends, we share a late supper and exchange gifts in honour of the King. The simple wooden-floored refectory is tastefully decorated as the coloured lights throw reflections on the faces as they who gaze in silent wonder at the face of God.

As I leave, the night is heavy with frost and the silver blue moon lights the yard before me. How blessed am

I that God has opened such a window for me. I have
sought God in many places, in many faces, in many
ways, and yet most of the time He lies hidden from me.
But every once in a while, when I least expect, I find
Him, hiding in the most unexpected of places – but,
more often than not, the real hiding place of God is the
human heart.

Acknowledgments

I have always loved the narrative style of story possibly because I have been inspired by so many people who give life to such stories.

This book would never have been possible without the help and encouragement of Ciara Considine, my editor at Hachette. Thanks also to Breda Purdue and all at Hachette. To Claire Rourke for copy-editing.

I would like to thank all those whose lives have inspired this book: Lya Vollering, Sr Rebecca Conlon, Dom Bruno Sullivan, The friends of Glendalough, Mutanu, The Poor Clare Sisters, John August Swanson, Kathy Levan, Fr Ollie Noonan and the people of Turkwell, George and all my friends in Medjugorje. The community where I reside in Graigcullen, Carlow, my colleagues Fr John Dunphy and Fr PJ. Madden, Kay, Suzanne, Rory, Clare, Josie, Isobel, Cathy and all at the Parish Centre Graigcullen. To Fr Brendan Byrne, Diocesan Administrator, whose support I greatly appreciate. And to the many people who have silently inspired me and whose amazing lives run through the pages of this book.

My colleagues in GIA, Chicago who publish the

music that gives life to many of these stories. To Mark Cahill my music partner and producer whose loyalty and insight are a true blessing. To Cathal, Martin, Brendan, Andy and Chris who give me reason to compose and perform.

To my family and friends who reveal so many hiding places of God each day without even knowing it. And, especially, to my parents May and Tom whose love and encouragement introduced me to my faith and much more and who have been a constant source of story for my life.

Finally I would like to acknowledge the support of all who continue to find a place in their lives and on their shelves for my music and words. You are the true source of all that enriches my life and work.